Twelve Months at Barclay Lake

Twelve Months at Barclay Lake

T. E. Trimbath

iUniverse, Inc.

New York Lincoln Shanghai

Twelve Months at Barclay Lake

iUniverse, Inc.

For information address:
iUniverse, Inc.
2021 Pine Lake Road, Suite 100
Lincoln, NE 68512
www.iuniverse.com

ISBN: 0-595-33114-9

Contents

Introduction

There are dozens of guidebooks describing hundreds of trails in the Cascade and Olympic Mountain ranges. There's a good reason for that. The area is beautiful. The mountains are young, so the rocky crags aren't worn down. They are along the Pacific Rim of Fire, so volcanoes poke up two miles high and get capped with glaciers. The air is wet with storms hitting land for the first time after their long trips across the Pacific. That weather brings tons of water for glaciers, snowfields, waterfalls, lakes and rivers. The trees love it and grow straight, tall, and magnificent. If the land was flatter or the weather milder, the entire area might be settled and paved. That can't happen though because there is a wildness to the area that is tougher than bulldozers.

I finally realized that I couldn't see it all.

For a while, I tried. For two decades, I hiked more often than most, though not as often as some. Sometimes I visited old favorites, but most of the time I explored. At the start, every trail was unknown and novel. Satisfying my curiosity was fun and almost every weekend was spent with a pack on my back. Eventually something bigger started to happen. I began enjoying how the views and valleys stitched themselves together in my head. Each new hike wasn't a separate event, but a peek at an overlooked corner of an immense playground. I enjoyed getting to a ridge and seeing other ones I had climbed, or finding a trail intersection in the forest that led off to some other familiar site.

As the list of unvisited hikes shrunk, deciding where to explore next took more time and energy. After two decades of hiking, the remaining trails were either too tough because they were long, steep, or far away, or they were too easy because they were short, flat, or so close that they were too busy. Choosing one and fitting it in was no longer a casual decision. It was either a concerted effort, or felt like a major concession. My trips became much more dependent on logistics, weather, my condition and my mood.

Something didn't seem right. Hiking a trail is something to do because I will enjoy it, not to check off another box on a to-do list or gain some bragging rights. I quit trying to hike every trail in the guidebooks and I went back to the core of why I enjoyed hiking in Washington.

The area is rugged and changes from rain forests, to old growth, to alpine meadows, to crags of rocks, snow and ice. That is why the trails are so varied. The variety is amazing. Everything from flat valley hikes to vertical ice walls is available. Seeing that variety fascinates me. Getting the view from the top of a ridge or peak is awesome. Finding more intimate settings like lakes hidden by ridges and fringed by trees is very special.

I had seen a lot of the area but I realized that most of what I knew was gained through single visits to lots of places instead of lots of visits to a few places. My memory of each of them was a mental snapshot of that location on that particular day with that specific weather. What were those places like at other times in the year? I could guess, but didn't know. I realized that I'd met those trails and destinations but I didn't really know them. That sparked my curiosity, which is always a dangerous and energetic event.

What were those places like on another weekend, or during the week? Then I began to wonder what they would be like throughout the year. The seasons drastically change the Cascades. Some places get almost a hundred feet of snow and then have near-drought conditions after it all melts.

I wondered if there were places that I could visit throughout the year. What would I see if I hiked to a place in the summer and skied there in the winter? Finding a place where I could do both without stupidly risking my life would be the hard part.

For me, the trick was knowing what I liked and where my limits were. Some folks could summit Mt. Rainier in almost every condition. I am much more pedestrian, but a lot of territory is open to me because I like to hike on snowshoes and skis. Some of my best trips have been one easy mile past the snowline. The crowds stop at the white stuff and I get the rest of the place to myself.

My fear of heights stops me at the vertical walls. I don't do technical climbing. Imagine my guide's surprise when I told him that on our way back down from the summit of Mt. Rainier. My ski skills are intermediate at best. I'm steady but slow so I'm less likely to get very far from the road. I am lucky enough to enjoy hiking all year round. I am not a fair weather hiker, but I am not stupid about it either. Hypothermia happens too easily, so I do my winter traveling prudently. Prudence is very limiting in a Cascade winter. Those are my boundaries but they are broad enough to give me a lot of territory to play in.

Backcountry skills weren't the only concern. The mundane task of parking my car would be one major consideration. If I couldn't park near the trailhead, I couldn't get me or my stuff there without extreme measures. I also wanted to be able to camp overnight. There had to be established campsites that didn't upset the Forest Service. I wanted a place that wasn't too difficult to get to. There was no reason to set extra hurdles on purpose. Weather would produce enough obstacles without any effort on my part.

By forcing myself to a monthly schedule, I would get my butt out of the house during those months when it is too easy to get wrapped up in yard work and chores, and during the holidays when it is easier to eat than exercise. That meant I would get to see every season, catch the transitions between them, and keep myself active.

When I first went through this mental exercise, my wife and I lived in Bellevue near Interstate 90. We were only minutes from downtown Seattle but what I liked was the total lack of traffic when I headed east into the mountains on a weekday morning. An hour's drive on the interstate got me to Snoqualmie Pass and another hour got me past the winter ski crowds. I like hikes that are quiet and uncrowded. I settled on exploring the area east of Cle Elum: the Teanaway river basin.

For each of the next twelve months I drove the two hours with my Cherokee filled with everything I needed for hiking, snowshoeing and skiing. Mountain weather is highly variable, so I didn't know what I would need until I got there. I dealt with dusty roads and crowds in the summer, and solitude and road closures in the winter. Within that area, I varied my destinations and explored anything interesting that my middle-aged body could get to. Immortal adolescents and old folks in denial have a lot more options.

After twelve months of dayhikes, overnights and a wide variety of weather I was done. I was surprised by how much my image of the area changed when I got to know it in its various moods. The area wasn't a collection of twelve destinations. I recognized it more as a land with a unique character. It definitely didn't get boring. Learning about one area made me realize how little I knew about all of those places that I had visited only once. Maybe a place that was nasty and buggy was excellent if I went back in the fall or when the snowpack was thick and skiable. Maybe that alpine meadow that was trashed by that youth group playing kickball was quiet, serene and recovering.

I was hooked. Where would I go next?

Commutes change and we moved north of Seattle to Bothell to avoid some nasty traffic. We were closer to Highway 2 (US2) and Stevens Pass: one of the few paved routes across the Cascade Mountains. I was somewhat familiar with the area, but there was a lot there that I hadn't visited in years. Finding a destination was tougher though. The land is much more rugged, the roads are skinnier, and the parking harder to find.

After looking over the maps and guidebooks, I decided to visit the Barclay Lake area. I heard conflicting stories about it. It was supposed to be beautiful and messy, easy and treacherous, a great place to hang out and not worth going to. That much confusion intrigued me. Unraveling the contradictions was more appealing than going to some utopia that everyone agreed about.

I never recorded my thoughts during my visits to the Teanaway. By the end of those twelve months, I knew that my experiences were worth the effort, but my memories didn't recall enough to tell the story. For my trips to Barclay, I decided to take a camera and a notepad. I wanted to see how much my thoughts and impressions changed over the year. Hopefully, this book captures much of that story, but as most hikers know, words and pictures are a small fraction of the experience. If cameras and books could capture the wilderness, television and movies would be completely different and there'd be no reason to lace up your hiking boots. I hope this book captures enough to give you some impression of what I saw, how I felt, and what I learned and also to point out what you can see, feel and learn in your own adventures.

What I Knew Then

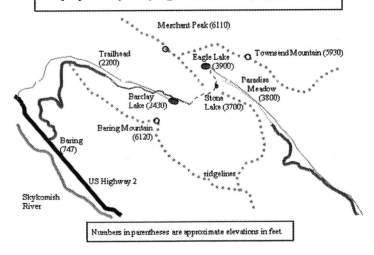

Sketch of Barclay Lake's neighborhood
Be prepared by carrying an accurate topographic map.

Merchant Peak (6110)

Trailhead (2200)

Eagle Lake (3900)

Townsend Mountain (5930)

Paradise Meadow (3800)

Barclay Lake (2430)

Stone Lake (3700)

Baring Mountain (6120)

Baring (747)

ridgelines

US Highway 2

Skykomish River

Numbers in parentheses are approximate elevations in feet

What I knew about Barclay Lake was based on two pages out of a 15 year-old guidebook, some half-remembered stories told by fellow hikers, and whatever I could gleam as I drove by on the way to other hikes.

Some of my ambivalence about Barclay Lake was because it was such a low lake that it wasn't even sub-alpine as far as I was concerned. It wasn't very far off the highway and was so close to town that some people passed it everyday as they commuted to Seattle. Of course, that's because Seattle's growth and traffic are creating incredible commutes. Supposedly, the lake got crowded. The trail to it was short, flat and easy, but the trail that led to Eagle Lake was a nasty hill climb up a brushy, messy, boot-beaten path that gained a lot of elevation in a very short distance. That didn't sound pleasant.

Barclay Lake itself didn't intrigue me as much as the area around it did. I like to pick hikes where I have to gain lots of elevation, sweat a lot and leave the crowds behind. That is where I expect to find expansive views from some ridge or peak with no one else around. A hike that didn't make me grunt left me feeling that I'd wasted my time. I liked doing something that felt significant. Barclay might not give me that, but I guessed that Eagle Lake and Baring Mountain could.

There was a back entrance to Eagle, but that was disparaged as a fisherman's trail and it was considered a cheat to use it. Barclay was described as an okay lake, but nothing special. In its defense, Baring Mountain, which was in the vicinity, was an impressive sight. It as an enormous thumb of rock with a split summit that is easy to spot from the highway. According to one report, climbing it was a walk-up. There was a path up the backside that led almost all the way to the summit. According to another report, it was unclimbable. I hoped the first report was right, but the second was more believable.

Guidebooks and maps gave me some data. Barclay Lake sits at 2,420 feet so it is below the elevation of the lowest mountain passes. That low it might not even get snowed-in often. The trail started at 2,200 feet and was only 2.2 miles long, so the grade was a nearly flat hundred feet per mile. Eagle Lake is at 3,900 feet and 1.5 miles farther, so that confirmed that the second trail was much steeper. Anything over a thousand feet a mile is grueling enough to act as a barrier to lots of folks. Baring tops out at almost 6,000 feet, which is amazing considering how low the surrounding valleys are. The highway runs beside it through a valley at less than a thousand feet.

There was more data available, but I knew enough to get started. I will read about a trail before I hike it, but the trail to Barclay sounded so pedestrian that I didn't worry the details. It was easy for me to trivialize the need for proper preparation.

One friend's story stayed with me. His small party hiked into Barclay and then tried climbing the trail to Eagle. They thought Barclay was okay, but nothing great. What really stuck with me, and what he spent the most time describing, was the failed trip to Eagle. The trail was hand-clawing steep, brushy, messy, and muddy. The rain and the water on the bushes soaked them and they turned back miserable. He wouldn't go back. I was willing to give Barclay a chance. If

Barclay didn't work, there were other places to try so I wasn't too worked up about it. For at least one trip, I'd try to keep an open mind and hope for the best.

October

Thursday, October 17

I was going to visit Barclay for twelve months. The best way the lake could make a good first impression would be for me to visit during a quiet day in the middle of the week during some fine autumn weather. Good weather and small crowds gave the place the best chance to show off.

I also wanted to see twelve typical months, but I knew that would be incredibly unlikely. Weather does weird things. Despite our images of the seasons and of the Pacific Northwest, sunshine happens in December and rain happens in August. The weather that October day was a good example. Normally the middle of October is the time for the first messy storms of winter. They come in windy, wet, almost cold enough for snow, and definitely chilly enough for pneumonia and hypothermia.

It was an atypically nice bit of October. It hadn't rained in a long string of days. The sky was clear and Seattle was forecast to break its record high temperature. That is perfect hiking weather.

For me the journey begins when I leave the house. Hikes usually aren't close to town, so getting there becomes part of the trip too. During the drive to the trail, I am fascinated with experiencing a cross section of the weather, the land, and the way we live there. My drive cut through densely packed civilization, slowly slid through thinning populations, and ended in near wilderness. The transition was amazing; and the fact that some folks never get out of the city, or conversely rarely go anywhere near town, makes me realize that I get a rare view of the world. That also meant that by the time I get to the trailhead my mind had been engaged for hours and miles. I keep in mind how difficult the hike would be without the aid of roads and cars. Would I make the effort if I had to use my bicycle instead of my car?

Despite that sense of wonder, I keep in mind that hiking is simply a voluntary luxury. Others might make it sound like much more. Because it involves a remote location and gear that can be bought in special stores, hiking takes on the feel of a specialized activity. I suppose to distinguish these hikes and make myself sound like an expert, I should maintain the image that hiking has some mystique and requires specialized equipment, learning and skill. Some people treat it like it is something apart from normal life. Get rid of that notion if it is keeping you off the trails. A hike is simply a walk. It is a walk that takes place outside and is usually not in the neighborhood. At its most basic level, it is using a skill you learned as a toddler.

Hiking shouldn't be trivialized though. Hikes are walks that happen where there is very little civilization. If something goes wrong, you have to be able to take care of it. But, the special equipment in a well-equipped pack is nothing more than some of the essentials that you should have in your car. If you remember that hiking is simply walking with a few things hung on your back, it can be less intimidating. I know people who want exercise routines for getting ready to go hiking. They worry about being ready and take classes. That is all right, but remember that if you can walk and carry a bag of groceries, you can go for a hike. Your first ones may take less time than it took to drive to the trail, but that will change as your body gets the idea that it will do this again.

Except for the lack of rain, the drive to the trailhead looked like a typical fall morning. There was fog in the valleys and the sun was just past the ridgetops and a little south of east. I had the heater on to take off the chill. The valley was won-derfully lit with muted autumn colors. The drive out along highway 2 was pretty enough that I could have spent the morning taking pictures of the river valley and farms backed by mountains. It was such a good idea that, sure enough, there was one guy setting up his tripod beside the river.

I knew to start looking for the turn about an hour from home. Luckily, there was a small sign for the Forest Service road. The turnoff was much more clearly marked than I expected. I turned, crossed two sets of railroad tracks, and passed a few small homes that made up suburban Baring. That put me on a gravel logging road.

The road was in good enough shape considering it was unpaved, and I didn't expect any traffic on a Wednesday morning. I could have driven uphill at full speed except for the lighting. It makes sense to slow down on logging roads. There is no way to know what trucks, cars, trees or potholes you'll find in the road and there is usually only a narrow lane and a half that rarely leaves room for maneuvering. The hairpin turns act as speed limiters too, but it was bright sun-shine and deep shade that slowed me down. The sudden lighting changes made such a great contrast that a simple shadow was enough to force my eyes to read-just. For a few seconds I couldn't see the road in front of me. I'd crawl into the shadows until I could see there wasn't anything in the way. It slowed me down but it was quicker than walking. The drive was steep and I caught on very quickly that the road was going to help me skip a lot of elevation gain. The road and my car did the work for me.

If the lake was a busy place, it would have a big parking lot. I expected a park-ing lot like the 200 car lots at some of the more popular places along I-90. That wasn't the case. The parking lot could probably hold less than a dozen cars. Did I have the wrong trailhead or did someone have a very odd idea of what should be considered crowded? Maybe people parked along the side of the road during the weekends. The only other car there was a subcompact. Almost every trailhead has some compact car or sedan parked at it. A few times they have left mufflers behind or gotten dings in their oil pans, but usually they get through. I was glad for my SUV and its ground clearance. It was one less thing to worry about.

Despite the glowing weather report, it was in the mid-forties when I got out of the car. A bit of shade and elevation can make a big difference in temperature. Even though everything should have been dried out by that year's drought, the ground, the plants, and the air were cold and damp. There were even bugs, which are usually dead and gone that late in the season. They didn't bite me, so I wasn't bothered.

I checked out the views from the trailhead to get a feel for the place. Straight ahead was the trail. Thousands of feet above it was Baring Mountain looking like a single spire of smooth sheer rock. Its base was hidden in the deep forest that the trail dove into. To my right was a heavily wooded and weedy hillside that I quickly ignored because it looked like someone tried terracing it for something but then abandoned their efforts. To my left through the trees the land fell away into a forest-filled valley. The opposite valley wall was a long broken ridge of craggy mountains that looked much rougher than anything I expected to see on such a low hike. The forest only managed to get halfway up the slope. Above that it was either too steep for trees, or so avalanche prone that every living thing was swept away each winter.

After years of lots of hikes, I've also become entangled in the gear and logistics of hiking. Besides the essentials that authorities dictate, I also take along other things that make the trip easier, safer, and more fun. My daypack is as large as some overnight packs and heavy enough for a good workout.

I put my pack, gloves and boots on, hung the trail pass on the rear view mirror, locked the car and started hiking. My impression of a too-pedestrian hike got modified. Most pedestrian hikes have extensive parking lots and restrooms and don't require trail permits or signing in at a register. Besides the trail sign and registration box, all I saw was a bunch of gravel and a path of packed dirt.

The trail led down from the parking lot. That isn't typical for most trails in the Cascades. Most of them start climbing as soon as possible. It flattened soon after it dropped into the forest. It was dark under the trees. I didn't need a headlamp or anything like that, but it wasn't the bright, cheery hiking conditions that had to exist on the south side of Baring. It was sunny over there, but I was in deep shade on a bright, sunny day.

It was a good trail, wide and packed enough for comfort. It obviously got enough traffic to get packed so well. Occasionally, a patch of plants stuck out into trail and tried to get my legs wet. They succeeded, but it wasn't much of an issue. I was surprised though. The weather in town had been so dry that I thought I'd find dust, not mud. Looking around I noticed that the moss was doing well enough to remind me of the Hoh rain forest. Something kept everything wet. I blamed the fog and dew that hid in the shadow of Baring Mountain.

Despite all of the moisture, the plants were wilting. The predominant color was a faded yellow with withered brown spots. For a while, I looked for a monster big leaf maple. The enormous leaves carpeting the trail had to come from somewhere. Then I realized the leaf I was looking at was from Devil's Club. Its leaves were more than a foot across. They come from a bush that dies back every year, but each spring shoves its way up through moist soils to become head-high stalks of thorns. The leaves and flowers are not a problem. Some people like them. But if Devil's Club became extinct, hikers would celebrate the disappearance of its spiny stem and its tendency to get mistaken for a handhold too late. Actually most hikers would mourn because we are a conservation minded lot and don't want species to disappear, but check my opinion again the next time I am picking thorns out of my palm. I've had to bushwhack through it and learned to avoid it. At least I wasn't hacking through it, so as long as it stayed out of the trail I wouldn't fight it.

There was some evidence of the dry fall. The streambeds were dry. A few held a trickle, but I have no idea where they got their water. It was late for snowmelt, so I probably splashed through old rainwater that was slowly working its way down the mountain. Water is one of the noisiest features in the Cascades, so without it the hike was very quiet and felt a bit lonely. My footsteps and the falling leaves were the noisiest sounds in the forest.

I accepted the drying out of the little streams that cross the trail. Most of them were less than six inches deep and are easy to step across. The big surprise was finding the main streambed exposed and dry. It was a twenty foot wide pile of rounded grey stones. It takes a lot to turn off a lake and drain its outlet. My first view of the grey rocky bed made me wonder if the lake would be a dried up puddle. That would be a disappointment. Hiking to a mud pit didn't sound appealing and would explain why the parking lot was almost empty.

The streambed was parched but the land under the trees was damp. The fog and dew were as effective as a good rain. The forest appreciated the moisture but it didn't make my life easier. The trail turned from a beaten dirt path to a highly irregular boardwalk that was wet and slick.

The boardwalk wasn't like those on some resort's beach. The boards were more like firewood. They were split from trees found along the trail. Each board was at least three feet long, about a foot wide and more than six inches thick. Some were smooth but most were ribbed and warped. They weighed more than I wanted to lift. Boardwalks are usually built over ground that will easily get trampled to mud or over terrain that is too uneven to build a trail through. Those boardwalks looked like the anti-mud type.

My gripe was that the split surface was worn smooth. Even the warps and ribs were slick channels that let feet slide to the side. A little moisture turned them slippery and hazardous. If they were level that wouldn't be too bad, but very little is flat in the forest. There was always a tilt, incline or twist to each section of trail, so any slip could send a hiker skidding down the boards and off into the bushes, rocks, mud, or Devil's Club. That wasn't life threatening, but a broken ankle is a tragedy to the person who owns the ankle. And a broken ankle is not an easy thing to manage on a trail. The worst part was the section of boardwalk that tried to maneuver down a slight grade between garage-sized boulders. The trail was a serpentine that had slumped and twisted enough to create banked turns. That might be fun on a mountain bike, but my hiking pace is way below the speed that could keep me up on a banked turn. Flat dirt felt as safe as getting back to a dock after a day of sailing.

The stretch of dirt was short and led to another construction project. The major stream coming out of Barclay Lake was recently equipped with an excellent log bridge with handrails and anti-skid crushed rock. It was long enough that there were center posts dividing the bridge into halves. The footbed was made from two logs laid beside each other. The gaps between the logs were filled with gravel. Another log made a handrail. It was a stout and fine bridge for crossing a stream. What was lacking was water in the stream. A bridge over a pile of rocks looks a little silly. A spring flood would change that point of view. In either case, the bridge was appreciated. The steep banks and the long bridge were evidence that the water would be back in a big way. Crossing the flooded stream would be dangerous without the bridge. I hoped the construction crew was able to take advantage of the dry conditions. Building a bridge over a stream without having to worry about getting wet is probably rare and very handy.

After I crossed the bridge and made the hairpin turn at the top of the bank I looked back. The bridge, streambed and trees made a nice little setting. The far bank held a collection of trees and leafy bushes that grew on and around the massive boulders. They were highlighted by the contrasting lightly colored rocks in the streambed. The footbridge tied the two shores together and added some rustic browns to the site. I liked the way the forest framed the stream and the way the light fell on the bridge. I also liked the random dead branch or scraggly bush that kept the place from being too perfect, too unnatural. The results were obviously too rough to be the product of a landscape architect. It would look better with water running through it though.

That was where the first patch of sunshine found me. Until then, any evidence of a hot fall day seemed a mirage. A bit of sunshine made an enormous and quick difference, so the jacket went into the pack and I took the opportunity to stop, have a snack, and soak up some warmth.

It was a quiet little place to relax. It didn't have any grand vistas or impressive wildlife. It was simply a nice bit of forest that was comfortable and pleasant.

When I started hiking again I fell back into my habit of eating up distance by keeping my head down and using my long strides. I can set up a rhythm that lets me move along the trail and cover a lot of ground so I have more time to spend at the destination. Distractions get tuned out and I concentrate on making progress.

I tuned out enough of the world that I almost had a head-on collision with the mushroom ladies. They were a couple of women that were wrapped up in conversation. I had my head down and wasn't thinking about much. The forest absorbs noises and none of us were paying attention so it was good and surprising that we somehow noticed each other before colliding. We apologized all around. They passed along a clean trail report and satisfied my curiosity about the shopping bags that they carried. Whenever they think the time is right, they head on up to Barclay Lake in search of small mushrooms that they called Angel Wings. Evidently, a third of bag was a small haul for them, so they were a bit disappointed. That didn't affect their mood though so I guessed that they weren't harvesting them for the money. Some folks who pick mushrooms for profit get testy about their business and I didn't want to broach the subject. They were probably getting something to throw into an omelet. They must have gotten there at dawn. I met them about a mile in from the trailhead, so by the time they got out and got home it would be way past breakfast. Maybe that was for tomorrow's omelet. We had a nice and sociable chat before we went different directions.

After that, I assumed I was on my lonesome.

The trail hadn't seemed very messy considering what I had been told to expect. The boardwalks were slicker than I liked, but the trail was well graded with no major mud puddles, and it didn't wander off in odd detours. The walk was pleasant and peaceful though a bit muted and subdued by the dampness and chill. It felt like October, which of course was very proper.

The trail also wasn't very long. A short while after talking to the mushroom ladies I was at the lake. I had been in head down mode so thoroughly that I don't remember much of what I passed. That was a bit stupid. It is a habit from my longer hikes. On a ten mile hike, I have less time to watch the world go by. I have to spend more time on progress and mileage, so I set my legs on automatic and worry more about looking for places to step and less about enjoying the view. I save the view time for the ridge or lake that I aim myself at. I'd have to adjust my normal speed; otherwise, I'd essentially run to the lake and run back to the car. Where's the fun in that?

Forests on the west side of the Cascade Mountains are thick enough that lakes can hide. It is easier to find the lake by looking up for gaps in the canopy, than to look for water through gaps between the trees. The gap in the canopy lets in light and is the first sign that the lake is near. The other thing that announces the lake is the campsites. At any lake worth a visit, campsites tend to get stomped into the flattest pieces of earth at the nearest shoreline. Usually that is at the outlet, but at Barclay Lake the trail takes its own course and approaches the lake at its middle. I came across campsites and saw light overhead. A few feet later, I looked between some trees and saw the beach and the lake.

The lake level answered any doubts I had about the dryness of the season. It was down enough that I wondered if it was being used for irrigation or flood control. Irrigation lakes aren't much fun to visit. Their shorelines become barren and ugly. Natural changes are overwhelmed by the effects of civilization. Luckily, that wasn't the case. Using Barclay for irrigation didn't make any sense. Western Washington is wet enough to not need it, and the lake wasn't big enough to water many people or acres. Barclay was down that far for simple seasonal reasons. There wasn't enough water flowing into the lake. I guessed that the water level was down by about six feet. The far end of the lake looked like a tidal mud flat. There should have been shorebirds and sea gulls walking along on it. The fish couldn't be too pleased. They were squeezed into about half the lake they had at the beginning of summer.

The lake was nice enough at first glance, but I was quickly distracted by the monumental view of the opposite side of the lake. It was hard to absorb the view of the immense wall that is the backside of Baring Mountain. Directly across the narrow measure of the lake and less than a mile away, it tops out at four thousand feet above the lake surface. Most of it proves Baring Mountain was given the right name. The top half is bare stone. The rock is vertical enough that great sections of it can't support soil or mosses. That is one impressive grey spire of clean, flat, vertical rock. Few lakes get that close to that much rock. I was more impressed when I saw the wide split in the summit. Half of the mountain looked like it could peel off in a good earthquake. The gap was wide and deep enough to swallow small warships from WWII. When that slab falls, Seattle will hear it.

Eventually I let myself look at the surrounding terrain. About two thousand feet below the summit and on its right was a ridge. The trail ran along its base, but I couldn't see it because it was hidden beneath the trees. From there, forest wrapped around the lake to cover the land and fill the valley. Directly below the sheer rock face of Baring Mountain were open talus fields that fanned out along the base of the mountain and touched the lake at its outlet. On the other side, to my left, was the lake's marshy end and the rest of the valley. It was more like a basin. High up on its walls were steep slopes cleared by avalanches. There, only shrubs lived. Somewhere in that basin was a hidden waterfall that kept the valley from getting too quiet but it too was hidden within the forest.

I sat down beside the lake. My chair was an enormous fallen log that jutted out over the beach. I wanted to sit still and give my mind time to absorb as much of the view as possible. It was overwhelming. The break was also an excuse to give my body a break before I headed up to Eagle Lake.

Rocks and trees are impressive but there were more active things around too. The fish were jumping and the spiderwebs were everywhere. There were probably a lot of bugs, but I didn't notice. Maybe there were lots of hungry fish and spiders.

The guidebook said that to find the trail to Eagle Lake, look for a small side trail past the last campsite at Barclay Lake. In other words, walk past all of the campsites, try to figure out which was the last one when the description was written, and then backtrack investigating all of the side trails. Invariably this meant finding and following too many trails that lead to bits of decaying toilet paper. Past the last campsite is always a maze of trails built by dashes into the bushes. I am somewhat unfair though. I suspected that the little four rock cairn I passed at the far end of the lake probably marked the correct path. Without any sign spelling it out, I decided to investigate the other possibilities. I would hate to turn at the wrong cairn to later find out that there was an actual printed sign just a little farther along. It wouldn't be the first time a cairn has led me wrong.

The side trail led away from the lake and started to climb within a hundred feet. Finding the second cairn gave me confidence. Cairns in a line meant I was probably on the right track to something. Another cairn or two went by and it was obvious the trail was serious about climbing. After the third cairn, the slope was steep enough that I was breathing hard and sweating. A few cairns later the way was marked with colored ribbons. I realized that lots of folks worked on making the trail easier to follow. Easier doesn't mean easy. There were places where I was lost for a bit and it took some time and luck to find the trail. The idea is that trail marks should be easy to see, but the gaps between them were long enough that a fallen tree or a faded ribbon broke the visual string. The thick undergrowth around the lake was gone, so it was easy to misinterpret the barren forest floor for a beaten footpath with needles on it. On the map, the trail is a dashed line and it lived down to that distinction.

One thing was definite. The trail is very straightforward about climbing the hill. It has about 1,500 feet to climb and it doesn't stretch itself left and right across the hillside with switchbacks. It went very nearly straight up the hill and only deviated to get around rocks, trees, and streams. I saw why some folks said the area was too easy and others thought it was too hard: different points of view based on whether they stopped at Barclay Lake or tried to get to Eagle Lake.

About halfway up the hill, I came across an old rockslide and a rare bit of open air. The opening in the tree canopy offered gorgeous views across to Baring Mountain and a good place to take a break. It was obvious that the side of Baring Mountain I looked at didn't get much sun. The little bit it had when I was down at the lake was all it was going to get until much later in the day. The sun had a long way to go to get around that peak. There were even a couple of large snow patches in the largest avalanche chute. They survived a summer drought that was severe enough to dry out the outlet stream. That was impressive. The upper meadows were definitely in the sunshine though. The blueberry bushes had enough leaves left to throw a lot of color my way. Where I stood looked pretty too, but the bushes are always prettier on the other side of the valley.

I got lost one or two more times. Sometimes the trail crossed a rockslide and dove back into the trees while I was looking for more cairns up on the rock field. Looking for cairns in a rock pile means looking for piles of rocks amidst piles of rocks. The trick is finding the ones built by hikers and not the ones built by Mother Nature. Occasionally I had to backtrack to find the route again. Thanks to everyone who placed those flags and cairns. Without them I would not have attempted the climb, or at least wouldn't have completed it, but a few more would be helpful.

I was glad and surprised to see Stone Lake. Memorizing guidebooks and maps is not something I do well. I'd forgotten about the lake. Stone Lake sits beside the trail amongst the trees near the top of the climb and is closely held by a small, high valley. The trail runs past the lake without any detours to obvious campsites or fishing spots. That may be because the lake is not a major destination. It does not have some grandiose setting with craggy ramparts above it or acres of meadows around it. It is more of a large pond in a quiet and comforting setting. It deserved visitors. As I passed by, it was mostly in shadow, but it hadn't lost its water like Barclay Lake. The backdrop was a ridge covered in blueberry bushes and sunshine. It was chilly in the trees though. I built up a good sweat on the climb and the temperature in the shade dropped enough to make me shiver.

According to the map, it looked like a reasonably flat trail from there to Eagle Lake.

As I stepped out of the trees above Stone Lake, the scene felt like something scripted for a movie or laid out like some corner of a theme park. There was a beautiful sunlit meadow with birds swooping through and a wonderful backdrop of a long open mountain ridge. It is surprising that it isn't part of some protected wilderness. Equally surprising is that someone hasn't built a resort here. If it was in Europe, there'd be signs to beer and bedding. All it needed was some deer wandering through for a high cuteness factor. A beer would have been nice too.

Instead of cute deer there were two old fishermen. They were on another trail that came out of the trees on the other side of the small meadow. Just like the guidebook said, I could find folks who only hiked about a flat half a mile to get there instead of the four miles and the fifteen hundred foot climb I had put in. Unless it is wilderness, logging roads cross through lots of the terrain of the Cascades. The official hiking trail is not always the shortest, flattest, or easiest route. Trails like the back door to Eagle Lake spring up from a convergence of a good destination, good enough roads, and a convenient place to park. I won't begrudge them the access. One man was 76.

I escape the crowds by hiking in the middle of the week. That is a rare privilege and I don't take it for granted. Solitude is good, but company can be much more entertaining. Despite the old adage, the three of us did not make a crowd. Besides, to continue hiking solo meant obviously standing around while I waited for them to get ahead, and then tracking them. That would be weirder than any awkwardness of imposing myself into their trip. Luckily, they were friendly folks and invited me along. Having a local guide made my life much easier. The trail through the meadow was harder to follow than the trail up from Barclay and I didn't want to spend more time wandering about in the mud. He knew the best way and I was glad to follow him.

We were all surprised at how wet the ground was. You could have convinced me that it was the rainy season instead of a drought. It was obvious that there was no official trail and it was obvious why that was the case. The ground was too messy. Packing down dirt to make a trail is easy and cheap, but packing mud is much more difficult. Building a mile long boardwalk across muck wouldn't be cheap or easy. Instead, we maneuvered along a web of trails that were lines of churned mud and trampled bushes. They all headed in the same general direction, but there was no organization to them. In decades of use, no one trail became the obvious best. As one trail got churned, people abandoned it and mashed down some more bushes to make a new path. When that got too bad, another was picked. The process is random and very messy.

We were in sunshine, but the season was wearing down. In the shade, we found quarter inch thick ice. That was much more than a heavy frost. Puddles had frozen, drained, and left their miniature skating rink behind. It won't take much for the snow to stick and the winter to set in.

There were two meandering webs in the meadow. The younger set was built as messy boots trampled muddy tracks while trying to avoid the older web. The streams created the older web as they drained the valley. Trapped between the two webs were open areas of grasses and flowers that were anchored by small tight stands of trees. Around the shores of those islands of trees were heather with wilted flowers. The meadow was a quilt of trees, shrubs and grasses stitched by brown trails and clear streams.

We wanted to take a straight line to the lake. People are linear that way. The streams took great meandering routes through channels that were deeper than they were wide. Most of them could be stepped across, but a few required a bit of a jump. The banks were crowned with vegetation except at the trail crossings where boots had worn the plants down to mud. It was all wet and slippery, so the jumps were easy to misjudge. The muddy paths responded by steering for this year's firmest ground and shortest jumps. Getting wet was a real possibility.

The edge of the meadow was surprisingly abrupt. There was one last stream that marked the border. The opposite bank was only two feet farther but it was under an old forest canopy that had very little undergrowth. We passed through a curtain of trees and were on dry land. The beaten path walked up a slight rise and we enjoyed the solid dry earth after the squishy meadow. Suddenly not having to worry every footstep was so relaxing. It showed how much work it took to keep our balance on the mud. A few hundred quick dry feet later, we were at the lake.

I had heard about a cabin at the lake. Before forests got organized people proclaimed an area worth visiting by planting a cabin beside it. The forests have been organized for a long time, so the cabin must be old. It made an obvious destination for lunch. We sat on the porch, opened our packs, and pulled out our sandwiches. It was about 1PM.

It was nice talking to someone who knew the local history. According to the eldest angler, a local family owns the cabin and has some sort of grandfather arrangement with the Forest Service. The family uses it and tries to maintain it, but the cabin is remote enough that it is effectively abandoned most of the year. Keeping it livable is tough. Mother Nature is harsh enough, but the vandals are worse. The front door was busted, so it was easy to see inside past a slashed screen door and a tattered cloth of a curtain. The porch was gouged and there were holes in the floor.

Despite the damage, the cabin should be there a long time. The cabin walls were built from hand-hewn logs that were about 8x12. It was probably old-growth lumber from back before anyone used that term. The roof wasn't doing as well and was lucky that the tarps were in good condition. Inside there was enough room for a couple of bunks, a small kitchen and a place to sit. That is luxury so far from the road. It looked serviceable, but I don't know whom you have to ask for permission to use it. I'm sure the local mice would be happy to have someone drop by for an evening.

I am a fan of wilderness and can be very comfortable and happy lying in my sleeping bag in my tent, but I understand the desire to have a cabin by the lake. I know a lot of hikers who get to a particularly beautiful spot and then say, "Wouldn't it be great to have a cabin here?" It looks like the answer is yes, but the upkeep looked immense. Owning a house in suburbia takes a lot of work. Maintaining a cabin in the wilderness can't take less. Well, I guess it can take less if you drastically drop your standards.

But then there is the European model. Instead of having a cabin at the lake, how about letting some business run a lodge there? Having a lodge at every lake, peak and ridge would be terrible. True wilderness is precious and should be protected. It is like virginity that way. Once it is gone, there is no getting it back. I like going where no one is around and there is no sign of civilization. Occasionally, a bit of civilization is a good thing. In a place or two that are close to town, it would be nice to only hike a mile or a few and find a beer and a bed at the end. I settled for a peanut butter and jelly sandwich and a seat on a battered wooden porch.

There was a lot of litter in front of the porch and someone left a mess inside the cabin. Rifle shells were scattered on the ground. I guess it was part of someone's constitutional rights to bear arms and maintain a militia. What were they shooting at? Were deer assaulting the front porch? Is that how they fished? Did the rocks look threatening? In any case, I wish they'd clean up after themselves.

After the history lesson, the two of them talked shop about their teaching careers. I asked a few questions and they were friendly enough, but I started to feel like it was time for me to leave them alone. As I finished my sandwich and got ready to leave, they got out their fishing gear.

I wanted to climb the ridge on the other side of the lake, but I had to get back for a class in town. It would have been marvelous to spend the night and have more time to relax and roam about. I'd try to fit that in within the next eleven months but suspected it wouldn't happen until the spring. My guess was that the lake wasn't very far from winter's assault and siege.

Leaving was harder than I expected. It wasn't an emotional thing. I simply lost the trail. On the way in, I was so wrapped up in the conversation that I hadn't paid attention to landmarks. It took me a couple of dead ends before I found a trail marker. Some more trail markers up at the lake would be handy for klutzes like me. After a while, I found familiar boot prints in the mud and hoped they were mine.

On the way out the weather held and the temperature was perfect for hiking. There didn't seem to be nearly as many mud holes as I remembered. A little knowledge of where not to go helped me stay on drier land.

My old, used, sore knees kept me from taking any great advantage of the downhill. The trail between the lakes was steep enough that most steps required some thought and planning. Stepping high to climb was easier than extending a leg for each step on the way down. The ski pole helped. I carry a busted ski pole as a walking stick. It is very useful for descents. I'll drop some of my weight on it first and then step down. My knees appreciate the effort.

Evidently, I wasn't the only one on the trail. I heard voices in the trees behind Stone Lake, but I never saw the people. If they were that far off the trail, they probably didn't want to be disturbed. As long as they weren't hurting anyone or trying to burn down the forest I didn't care, but I will admit to being curious.

Back out on the rock field I was glad that I took pictures on the way up. Baring's mid-day shadow darkened everything below me. There was light along the ridge, but everything else was hidden in shadow and colorless. I looked across at a silhouette: a cardboard mountain. It was impressive but most of the shots were gone.

Finding the trail on the way down was easier than following it up. For the most part the way down was a blur. I plugged away at it, focused on route finding until I was back down at the little four-rock cairn beside Barclay's last campsite. My knees were glad to be back on level ground.

I didn't spend much time at the lake. Resting sounded like a good idea, but while I was gone, Baring's shadow filled the valley making it dark and cold. The spot where I first sat by the lake felt more gloomy than refreshing. Under the trees, it looked like night was falling. I knew better. For the fun of it, I got out my smallest single LED flashlight. It actually managed to light a patch of the trail. I didn't need the extra light, but I was surprised to see how dark it really was. There was no need for sunblock, but another warm layer would have been welcome.

The hike out was quiet and I was contented. Without the creek running, sometimes the noisiest thing in the forest was a falling leaf. It was a peaceful end to a very busy day. My mind needed the time to relax and absorb lots of new experiences and insights. My body would get to rest back home.

My hike took six hours; just like the guidebook said. How often does that happen? I am usually back at the car in less time than their estimate. There were three other cars in the lot. One was a new Saab with high performance tires that did nothing for its ground clearance. It looked like it wanted to be on a racetrack somewhere. I hope their undercarriage wasn't dinged.

There was a significant mix of experiences on the trail. The part to Barclay was flat and easy. The part to Eagle was a major grunt. When the sun is shining, the area has a lot to offer: the big wall of Baring, a few quiet lakes, blueberries, campsites, fishing and other wildlife. In the shade or near the trash it can be depressing. The bullet casings and broken glass around the cabin were the worst. Maybe the cabin acts like a magnet. Litter is also worst at the end of the season. I don't know where it goes in the winter, but all summer long litter builds along almost every trail I know and seems to be gone in the spring. Maybe mice use it for nesting material. I hoped I'd seen the trash at its worst and that the rest of the year would be better. I assumed that someone besides the squirrels and birds would pick it up.

The area around Barclay Lake was a better choice for the next year than I thought it would be. I had hoped for someplace that might be a bit better than average. It definitely met that criterion with the view of Baring. Everything else was a bonus. Barclay was pretty. Eagle was nicer than I expected. I looked forward to the pristine stillness of winter and the colorful flowers in the spring. There were a few negatives, but the positives were much greater and would keep me busy exploring and enjoying.

Deciding to visit some place for twelve months is easy. Seeing it through is the hard part. Nothing guarantees that life, fitness, and forest conditions will always line up to allow that many visits. Parts of it might not be accessible until the spring. It wouldn't take much snow to block the road. That hill climb to Eagle Lake in mid-winter would be much too much of an adventure for me. That marsh at the inlet could breed enough mosquitoes to keep people away for months. I wouldn't know that until I tried getting there throughout the next year.

I drove home looking forward to the next eleven months of hiking.

November

Wednesday, November 27

It was such an odd fall. There were long periods where we got to see the sun and didn't have to worry about the rain. That is not normal around Seattle. After October passes, the rains usually come in and stay until mid-July. Pessimists dread the grey skies. Optimists, or at least the skiers, hope it's cold enough for lots of snow in the mountains. A good snowpack also means a good water supply and no rationing. It was the end of November, almost Thanksgiving, and there wasn't enough snow in the high country to go rock skiing. The downhill ski areas were worried and the skiers and gardeners were bummed.

Bad weather for the snowpack was good weather for hiking. I had an excellent and rare opportunity to do some dry weather hiking in November.

Benign weather was nice, but it didn't keep the days from getting shorter. It was less than one month until the solstice. There wasn't much daylight to play with, and the sun didn't get much of a chance to warm up the air. The sky was clear and blue. There was frost in town.

I looked forward to a nice, short, relaxing hike to Barclay Lake. If I felt spunkier after I started hiking I could always step it up a notch and try for Eagle Lake too. That would be the limit though. There wasn't enough daylight for me to climb the ridge above Eagle.

As I turned from the highway and the Jeep climbed up to the trailhead, I rounded a corner and found a frigid and beautiful setting. Thick frost coated a crystalline pocket microclimate. Within a hundred yards, I went from late dry fall to some Christmas card setting and then back into fall. Maybe ice ages start in hollows like that. The trailhead parking lot was frosted too. The trail signs were wrapped in plastic for the winter. I felt like I stumbled into an area that was lonely, forgotten and abandoned for the season. I was alone.

When I got out of the car, shivers and goosebumps told me to dress for winter. Blue sky and sunshine looked great but the trailhead was in Baring's shadow. It was early in the morning. The sun was behind the mountain and didn't look like it would rise high enough to light the valley. As I got on the trail, I wondered if this little corner of the world would be in perpetual shadow until late spring. With the sun so low in the sky during the winter, the trail could be in the shadow for months. There might be nothing to melt the frost in that sunless nook.

Not everything was frigid. Most of the forest was dark and wet. It hadn't rained, so anything that got wet found the moisture in fog and dew. The dampness persisted. The lack of sunshine never gave things a chance to dry out. The forest felt closed in, like windows and doors shuttered against an approaching storm. But there weren't any windows or doors, just the plants that tightened their pores and the animals that stuffed their burrows.

The trail was wet, but not muddy, only messy. My boots got wet, but my toes were dry. Brushing against a bush was a way to get wet sleeves and pants so I was glad for good gear. One benefit was that the trail was more open than in October. Little of the shrubbery remained. Most of it was dying back and shriveling away from the trail.

While that could sound dismal and dreary, it was actually quiet and peaceful. I walked slower because I knew there was no rush on such a short hike. The peace and my pace gave me the opportunity to quiet my mind as I moved along. Sometimes that is a greater gift than the view or the exercise, and is one reason I can enjoy hiking alone. The mind needs time to relax and coast along. Too many distractions steer and drive it too hard. Hiking alone is not meditation, but getting into that rhythm of motion lets my mind ease. It can drift to whatever topic suits it and linger there until it casually drifts to the next. It is not the state of no mind, but is the state of free mind. Unfortunately getting into that situation is difficult back where there are roads and noisy neighbors. Sometimes my hikes are less about seeing nature and more about doing nothing. I find it odd and sad that all of our attempts at making things better, improving our quality of life, make it more difficult to find peace and quiet. I guess I proved to myself long ago that it takes less to find a better life, not more. Maybe that makes me abnormal; but my friends already told me that.

The trail was safe, but the boardwalks were treacherous. A little moisture slickened the wood and the thin moss. I wished I had worn mini-crampons for traction.

Boardwalks aren't on every trail, only those trails that get too much traffic through too fragile land have a chance of getting them installed. Unfortunately, a zero friction coefficient meant that the walkway that protected the land made life more dangerous for me. Pardon my excursion, but I stepped into the mud when I thought it looked safer than the boards. Trampling nature is bad, but breaking an ankle is bad too. Besides, in the middle of the week at the end of November there was no one else on the trail who could help me hobble out. Search and Rescue wouldn't have had a hard time finding me, but if they got called, it would disrupt a lot of their lives and cost a lot of money. The gas spent getting people to the trailhead would be a far worse environmental impact than a bit more trail erosion. I muddied my boots and apologized to the dirt.

A variety of environments passed by as I hiked. Much of the forest was dark with wet bark and soil. The leafy green bushes that brightened the undergrowth were fading. There were gaps in the canopy where a large tree had fallen. In those small glades were more of the sudden powdered sugar microclimates. Their sharp white crystals were a great contrast against the dark green forest. Fallen leaves had so much frost that the leaf was hard to see. The frost had the right shape and a bit of the autumn color; but spiky white dominated and turned leaves into frigid prickly pears. The frost was so frail that a casual touch melted it. The various frozen pockets looked like undiscovered art treasures because they were flawlessly frosted, pristine and obviously untouched. The mosses and the remaining berries maintained splotches of color at random intervals for a bit of relief. It was all one big forest, but it was not one big bland bit of dull green.

Evidently, the season hadn't been completely dry. Some rain came through, though far less than usual. But it was enough to start Barclay Creek flowing. The water was fresh and clear. As it ran over smoothed pebbles and around downed snags it changed the forest from quiet and peaceful to noisy and calming. I felt better because it looked and sounded more normal. I look for new things, but am comforted by what is familiar.

The boardwalks had been nasty, but the bridge was easy to walk on. It was frosted over too, but an ingenious work crew had spread sharp pebbles across its surface for traction. I thought about carrying a bag of sharp rocks for those boardwalks. That would be a very big bag of rocks. That didn't sound like a good idea.

After the footbridge, the trail walks along the opposite side of the valley. I found bits of sunshine as the trail hovered along the edge of Baring's shadow. I got to the lake just in time to catch a last glimpse of the sun before it passed behind Baring. For that moment, the lake was in shadow and I stood in sunshine on the shore. The opposite shore was frosted white. For a few minutes, the sun warmed me. Then, as it moved behind Baring, I turned and watched the shadow walk into the trees behind me and then climb the hill. My eyes followed it up and noticed that most of the climb to Eagle Lake looked warm and sunny. I also knew that by afternoon it would be dark, and if it was wet, it might be icy.

I stupidly left behind two essentials: a watch and a headlamp. That, and a desire to get home safely, made me cancel any plans to go farther. That was a disappointment. I had enough energy and wanted to see if the valley above had changed. Was last month's ice in Paradise Meadow the hint that Eagle would be frozen in November? I didn't want to extend myself to find out and wind up hiking down from Eagle in the dusk and then the dark. Instead, I decided to relax at Barclay and investigate its shoreline.

It was obvious that a lot of people camp at Barclay. Why not? It looks like a good family hike. It is fairly close to town, short, and flat relative to places up the highway. Some of those trails are three thousand foot climbs along miles of trails. Some families can handle such expeditions, but most are happy enough keeping it simple. Along the shoreline were lots of campsites beaten into the earth and that meant lots of little trails to explore. Most of the trails did nothing more than lead to other campsites, water, or private spots in the bushes. Enough led somewhere interesting though, that I enjoyed exploring and learning what others have found. The ones leading to pocket beaches were the best.

The outlet is not a simple funnel of narrowing shoreline or a waterfall's notch cut into bedrock. Instead, the water flows out through a porous rock dam built from boulders. The crowning boulder was as large as a truck. Barclay looks like it was formed from a massive rockfall from Baring. Where rocks have fallen once they can fall again. Thinking about that while standing on the pile of boulders was a bit unnerving, so I thought about other things. The rocks bordered a wide beach area that looked great for parties, but it was too uneven and natural to be used for things like volleyball games. Between the rocks and the beach was a logjam of driftwood far larger than any campfire needed. Entire trees piled up in a raft of grey wood logs as much as three feet in diameter.

The lake was refilling, so the Baring side of the lakeshore was underwater and inaccessible. There was no obvious route across the rocks and logs. I couldn't see a trail on the far side so there was no place to go if I managed to cross. I'd have to circumnavigate it some other season. On the near side, there were a couple of little coves with sandy beaches. The coves were a bit larger than individual campsites. Whoever camped there had a beach, privacy, and a bit of the lake to themselves. A little farther along was the rocky outlet that provided the best view of the lake by climbing the dump truck-sized rocks.

The beach definitely lacked tropical breezes. That season was gone and winter was near. Everything was cold in the shade of Baring. The first thin, feathery and fragile ice was forming in the coves. Maybe that bit of sunshine I saw on the shoreline earlier didn't make it down to that part of the lake. Even the sand was frozen and made odd crunching noises as I poked around the shoreline. Frozen ground crunches too, but the frozen sand had much taller ice crystals, so each step had that much farther to fall before it hit solid ground. With a bit more cold and not much more precipitation, maybe I could go ice skating. Would that happen in December?

In October, there were lots of mushrooms and fish. In November, almost everything was still. The waterfall provided the background noise and a rockfall added a bit of percussive accompaniment. Aside from that, even my own voice seemed too loud and passing planes were intrusive.

I didn't stay much longer. Without a watch, and with slippery trails ahead of me, I decided to head back. I didn't see anyone on the trail.

At a place that supposedly got swamped by crowds, I was able to find solitude and peace through a bit of timing and luck. My trip out was an opportunity to let my mind drift along enjoying the serenity without specific thoughts or observations intruding. That experience is the hardest to describe and the most precious. I was glad to find a place where that could happen.

It is a privilege to see places like that so late in the typical hiking season. Many places get locked away by snow every year and they only get visited by exceptionally hardy souls. It was nice to be able to watch the transition to winter at a place that didn't require an expedition. Everything was settling in and calming down, waiting for winter's main events. The plants and animals were beginning to drift into a long almost dream, accepting of the inevitable change and keeping one eye half-open.

December

Monday, December 30

It is easy to forget about hiking during December. The weather doesn't encourage it and the holidays swamp whatever free time pops up. Finally, after Christmas my to-do list shrunk. All of the presents were delivered. All of the cards were mailed. All of the baking was done. It was the day before New Year's Eve. The holidays had been fun, and I needed a nice quiet break.

Since November, the ski areas shifted from closed to busy. Those few weeks turned the slopes from bushes and rocks to a snowpack several feet deep. The Pacific weather factory fired a string of storms at Washington and one passed through that morning. I didn't want to deal with high winds. In the previous storm, we'd lost a thirty foot maple in our front yard. On the trail it could be much worse. The trees are bigger there and I didn't want to have to dodge flailing branches and toppling trunks.

The drive up was more of an adventure than the clear and dry days of the fall. Chains were required in the pass. Down in town was heavy rain. Somewhere between the two, the road would be slush. If I was lucky, the slush would be on the logging road, not the highway. In either case, I expected snow would keep me from driving to the trailhead.

The slush showed up on Highway 2 halfway through a big sweeping turn where I was passing a more sedate driver. The road went from wet to slush within less space than it took to pass a car. I was into four wheel drive and winter driving within seconds. It was embarrassing and dangerous to pass someone and then have to slow down. His reaction to the slush was more severe than mine. He bled off so much speed that I ended up with plenty of elbowroom, a jolt of adrenaline, and a holiday gift of a bit of guilt.

A few miles later at the turnoff, I slowly edged off the highway and stopped to look up at the snowline. A few hundred feet above me, the trees turned from green to white.

I found a hint of trouble before I got up there. Past the houses and less than a hundred feet along the logging road, a pond overflowed its banks and crossed the road. After splashing through the runoff, and being thankful for my car's ground clearance, I noticed that there weren't any tire tracks ahead of me. Evidently, no one had been up there since the last snowfall. With the morning's storm that might only be saying that I was the first one in the last few hours, but the place felt emptier than that.

The mix of snow and slush wasn't enough to hide the gravel. I gauged the snow depth by looking at my tracks in the rear view mirror. At the bottom of the hill, the tires threw the snow off the road and gravel showed through. A bit higher and the tires left two muddy lines through a slushy carpet. Above that and into the switchbacks the tracks were dirty snow that would probably melt if the sun came out. I steered around and bounced over fallen branches almost continually. Many of the limbs touched both sides of the road and lots of them were as thick as baseball bats. There wasn't any great danger as long as I drove slowly and carefully, but there also wasn't any reason to stupidly put a hole in my oil pan. Eventually, the tracks became solid white. I kept going, but slowly. The drive took long enough that I was convinced the trailhead was near. That became moot. I stopped when the back end and the front end of the car no longer agreed on which way to go. Neither seemed to care about what the steering wheel and I had to say about it so I stopped.

On New Year's Day a decade or so earlier, a hiking friend and I drove far into the hills on the north side of Mt. Rainier. We wanted to find the limits of his car and the edges of our comfort zones. We came across a car frozen to the snow about when we were ready to quit. It took about thirty minutes but we chipped away the snow and ice that had frozen to their car's frame. They were freed and headed home. Ten minutes after they drove off and as we felt pleased with ourselves, we found that his SUV was stuck. While rescuing the other car, his SUV's frame froze to the snow. Either it wasn't as bad, or we were better motivated, because we managed to free up his much heavier vehicle in less time with fewer people. It felt great when those wheels bit and gained traction. We turned around and went home.

As I drove to Barclay, I pictured myself trying to do the same thing ten years older and without his help. That was a bit of adventure that I did not want to repeat on my own. I started back down the hill. There was a bright spot. If there was enough snow for the car to slide on, there was enough for me to ski on.

I drove backwards for less than a quarter mile and found a spot wide enough to turn around in. Most logging roads around there have that fine pair of opposing features: a hill to run into opposite a cliff to fall off. I cautiously turned the car around so I wouldn't get to meet the hill or the cliff. The drive down was not easy. Touching the brakes started a skid. I stopped that and shifted down into a slow steady crawl down the hill. Patience and first gear go together.

I parked the car where the snow was reasonably skiable and the car was unlikely to get snowed-in. It was also within hiking distance of the highway in case anything bizarre happened. I've returned from other ski trips to find eight inches of fresh snow and a much tougher drive out. Of course, if things got that snowy I could ski down to the town of Baring.

All of that effort was just to go for a hike. So much for hiking being a simple and easy activity. Getting there is adventure enough sometimes.

When I left the house, I didn't know what to expect so the car was cluttered with gear for hiking, snowshoeing, and skiing. Playing around in Washington's mountains taught me to be ready for anything. Most of that gear lives in the car. The skis are about the only things that get added in the morning.

I hoped that the snow would be good enough for skiing. Making snowmen was a better use for what was there. The snow was packed tight and solid. On the bright side, two inches of hard packed base can be a lot better than eight inches of powder on a base of branches and rocks.

Getting ready for the first ski trip of the season always takes extra time. The sun hat gets put in the closet, and the thick jacket, hat and gloves go into the pack. That is, they go in after I spend time rummaging around looking for them. Invariably something gets left back at the house. I left my sunglasses back home. Thankfully, the clouds were doing a fine job of filtering the sunshine. I also spent time learning how to use some of my Christmas presents. Somehow, simple things like ski poles have become complicated enough to come with instruction manuals.

The weather couldn't decide if it wanted to rain or snow. The trees cast their own vote by dropping snowy hand grenades on everything. Wet snow that accumulated in the branches gradually melted into heavy piles. Randomly, clumps of snow the size of grapefruits fell from the trees and landed with a FUMP. It was definitely a good day for a wide brimmed hat, or maybe something tougher like a pith helmet. Ah, skiing in Western Washington is not the stuff of glossy brochures. It has its own style that has far more to do with slush than powder.

December days are short enough and my drive to the trailhead took a lot of time. There wasn't much day left. My hopes of making it to the lake faded. I didn't want to quit though, so I set my sights lower. I hoped to get to the trailhead. If things went well, then I'd see about getting to the lake, but I doubted that would happen.

I lost track of exactly how far I was from the trailhead and the highway. Driving makes it so easy to ignore distance. There is nothing like using your feet to learn how long a road is.

Back up the road I trudge skied. Forget what the tourism and recreation industries tell you about cross-country skiing when you hear me mention skiing. I was on cross-country skis, but what I did was not elegant. Those ski machines in gyms or in people's basements don't have a setting for slogging. Skiing uphill on a snow-covered, lowland, logging road is step after step of planting a ski, gaining traction, shoving the next one forward and repeating the process. It wasn't much faster than walking in slippery slush on long skinny snowshoes. I was sweating and moving slowly.

Why trudge up the hill like that when I didn't think I would make it to the lake? That wasn't my first winter ski trip where I skied a road instead of hiked a trail. It is part of being flexible and accepting changing conditions. I work with what I have.

Along the way I've learned that roads aren't bad. When we drive on them they are muddy or dusty and easy to dismiss. They are terrible things to walk along when traffic bounces by. When I've used road that were closed or abandoned I noticed that roads and trails are basically the same things. They are long narrow slices of civilization or an artificial scar through nature depending on your point of view. We create them to give us access to the forests. Terrain, budgets, logging and other interests decide whether there is a road, a trail, or an untouched forest. Only in wilderness areas and parks does an area's beauty affect the decision. Granted, trails are much less invasive, but they are merely narrow roads without cars. Some even have asphalt. A trail is an extension of the road with a parking lot at the junction. If the trailhead was originally built a mile closer to the highway, would the first mile of the trail be no good? There's usually something to see along the road, but in our cars we blast right by and can't even try to notice what's there. The nature on the roadside of the trailhead is usually the same as the nature on the trailside of the trailhead. There is one major distinction; trails get to much more interesting places. Roads can't follow those skinny, steep routes to hidden spots and marvelous views.

So for me, snow covered roads become wide trails. When I ski, the wider the trail the better. All of that extra room is a luxury, especially because I am a klutz and a lousy skier.

I wanted to get to the lake, but if I didn't, the road I skied on would undoubtedly show me something unexpected. I'd driven through that bit of forest a few times and I knew that skiing it would be a much better way to see the area. When I am driving, if I think about the scene outside, I guess it is a quiet country wood. The road keeps me occupied enough that I don't have enough time to think otherwise. The sights go by quickly and the sounds are overwhelmed by tire, engine, and heater noises. I get to see and hear much more on foot.

My trip up the road wasn't in silence. The skis weren't completely quiet and the highway added background rumbles for a while. Despite that, the sounds in the woods were much more noticeable. Completely randomly, and almost continually, trees back in the forest dropped dog-sized clumps of snow. As the branches sprung back up they threw off more snow to add a slushy, clumpy drizzle to the weather. Those grapefruit-sized clumps hitting me on the road were tiny in comparison. When I stopped long enough for my heavy breathing to ease, I heard not only the big snow clumps hitting the ground, but also the smaller cascades of snow falling through branches and the ever-present meltwater dripping from leaves and needles. Water made an orchestra of noises as it moved and melted.

The first part of the climb was between my own tire tracks. It was a moment-by-moment review of my driving technique. That was dull, but luckily the world around me was more interesting.

The first few seconds of every break were spent catching my breath. While my lungs caught up and rested, I looked around. The thickness of the forest impressed me. Establishing that first trail, then building the road must have been an enormous feat. I don't care if heavy machinery was involved; that was a lot of wood to move and a lot of dirt to flatten and pack. The remaining forest was thick enough with trees that, even without undergrowth, it was hard to see very far into the woods. A herd of elk could be a hundred feet away and I wouldn't know it. A cougar could be tracking me and I would be oblivious. Without undergrowth though, what could live there? Weren't the only foods pine cones and mushrooms? That sounded like fodder for squirrels and birds and it must have been enough. They would attract something that would eat squirrels and birds. I couldn't know for sure. The area was devoid of any evidence of animals.

Keeping my head down and working my legs hard, it seemed like I'd get to the end of my tire tracks soon. Soon didn't happen soon enough. I had driven much farther back down the hill than I thought. Either that or I was skiing much more slowly than I realized. What seemed like a short drive from the highway to the trailhead was much longer when my feet were getting me there. My tire tracks kept going and my energy reserves kept shrinking. It would be embarrassing to stop below the end of my tire tracks.

Eventually my tire tracks began to swerve a bit and I knew I was near their end. Where I turned the car around, I left a nice symmetric, almost artistic, set of tracks. The snow was deep enough that the tracks were clean and white, so there was just this nice, clean pattern in the snow. I laughed at how worried I had been about the car sliding over the edge. The tire tracks were far enough back that someone could have driven around me if I parked broadside in the road. Oh well, better cautious and silly than stranded and abandoned. Imagine waiting for months and the spring melt to call in a wrecker to pull a banged-up SUV back into civilization.

My clothes were soaked from sweat on the inside and a hypothermic drizzle on the outside. My workout was enough to keep me warm but, despite space age fabrics, I got chilled quickly whenever I stopped. I took shorter breaks and hoped they were enough.

Above that spot I expected to find clean unbroken snow, but instead I found someone's older ruts. Because it was early in the season, I suspected the ruts were soft enough mounds of slush for me to ski through. Later in the season, I would be more worried about ruts freezing and becoming death rails for my skis. Frozen ruts worry me when I ski on mixed-use roads. Some skiers don't like snowmobiles because of the machine's noise and smell, or because a few drivers are rude and dangerous. Skiing on mixed-use trails is akin to bicycling on a busy street. I know I can manage that though. I safely bicycled across the United States. In both cases, I mourn the loss of peace and quiet. My concern with snowmobile traffic is the danger posed by their ruts. In almost any snow condition, but definitely after things consolidate, the ruts become channels that trap skis. Without the ability to turn a ski, a skier can't control speed or direction. I've used lots of ibuprofen and had lots of bruises and injured joints from sharing tracks with snowmobiles. I felt bad about my car's ruts and hoped that the snow would stay soft enough for my trip down.

Down in that stretch of the road the forest is second or third or fourth growth timber growing so closely together that it is hard to tell what the terrain is like. After the road switchbacks a few times, gaps in the trees open up and I could see the land fall away. There is a valley out there but the trees tried to hide it. The clouds helped the trees hide the view. The valley was filled with weather. Occasionally the mist thinned enough to allow a ghostly image of the far side of the valley to show through. If I hadn't been there before I would have been more impressed with the rock walls wearing new snow, but I knew that I was missing an even more impressive show: the view of the crags on the ridge top. The opposite side of the valley is steep and wore a new white face. Smooth rock walls hadn't shed the snow yet, and the canopy of trees showed more white than green. Rare glimpses through the clouds showed peaks camouflaged in white. Without trees or bare rocks, it was hard to distinguish between cloud and terrain. Baring only showed one bare shoulder and that jutted out like a prime site for a forest fortress. It was vertical and square with a border of trees below it. Behind it was a hint of where the mountain could be, but that was more imagined than real.

I was glad I didn't drive any higher. The snow got deeper and the ruts became erratic squiggles. Evidently, the driving had not been easy. Only one set of tracks made it to the trailhead. Luckily, they managed to get back out again. That doesn't always happen. It seems that every year I come across at least one truck or car stuck up some logging road for the winter. They usually don't fare too well from a season's weather and vandals. The local mice probably enjoy such a nice, safe condo so at least something good comes from it.

The highway noise was long gone. The sound of snow falling from branches was accompanied by running water. The weather switched between snow and rain a few times and settled on a constant, cold, soaking drizzle: pneumonia weather as a friend called it. Except for the occasional branch on the road, I didn't see any major evidence of the windstorm, but my nose told me something big had fallen. The scent of freshly turned earth was very strong. Some large tree must have been uprooted and exposed a crater of fresh earth that hadn't seen light for decades. There were probably some surprised earthworms too.

The idea of skiing to the lake might be a fine adventure for some, but it was outside my comfort zone. At the trailhead the snow was deep enough for skis, but the trail was a very sloppy mix of snow and mud. There wasn't enough snow to ski on and I suspected the rest was a slippery mess.

The real reason I stopped was that I was beat. The work getting uphill left me with very little energy. I had enough time and energy to get back down from the trailhead, but adding a round trip to the lake was pushing it too far.

I consoled myself with the hope that January would bring better snow and a bit more daylight.

Barely getting to the trailhead confirmed one of my suspicions. The road might be blocked for the winter. For the next few months, snow might force me to park closer to the highway and make much longer trips. The snow-covered road seemed odd considering the low elevation of the lake, but microclimates happen and the area around Baring was always chillier than the forecast. I was disappointed that I wouldn't get to see the lake throughout the year. A similar thing happened in the Teanaway though. That road was closed for months. I managed to enjoy the trips though by breaking my prejudice against hiking on roads. The road to Barclay passed through interesting land that was worth exploring. It is easy to ignore the beauty of an area once a road goes through it, but it is also easy to ignore that pavement when it is covered in snow.

I turned around to head back down to the car. Early snow like that can be sticky or slippery and I didn't know how hard it would be to go downhill. At the top, it was easier than usual. Gliding downhill to the car felt decadent. Farther down the hill, the snow began to stick. The decadence didn't last long. The ride downhill was easier and faster than the climb, but the snow stuck enough that I had to kick to keep going. I wasn't sliding downhill, but I wasn't trudging either. I was in the middle, having to work a bit to slide a bit. The little breeze in my face brought on an impressive wind chill. I had three layers on already, but added a fourth for wind protection. After that, I was downright cozy: sweaty, but cozy. That is a very familiar scenario in a Puget Sound winter.

Before I got to the car, the snow started to melt and thin. If I kicked too strongly or used a slight edge for a turn, the skis ran through gravel. This is nothing new for me, but it can be a nuisance and usually threw me into an ungraceful stumble. Those were my rock skis and they lived up to their name. I've walked them across so much gravel that they might as well be covered in sandpaper.

With a bit of caution and a wince or two, I got back to the car. Ah, one of the glories of going out alone is that no one sees you fall.

Why didn't I bring a change of clothes? It was a treat to ski back to within a few feet of the car. When I got there, I was soaked and ready to get home.

Steam came from me and everything I wore. My boots became two little chimneys after I took them off. Eventually everything got thrown into the car. The windows got so fogged up that there was no rush to get to the highway. Why drive when I couldn't see where I was going? I sat there for a while listening to Christmas songs and letting the car's de-humidifier work its heart out. Occasional barrages of snow hit the roof. It felt good to be inside and safe after such a good, though hypothermic, workout. One of the joys of playing outdoors during the holidays is getting warm and cozy again while enjoying Christmas goodies. I poured myself some nice tea and worked my way through cookies and maple syrup candy while the internal fog faded.

I'd missed the lake, but that was part of what I wanted to learn about the area. When does the weather set in? How accessible is the area in different conditions? Do lots of folks try to get there throughout the year or is it only me? I was learning about the complete environment and that was the whole idea.

If the snow stayed and more storms came through, the skiing might be better but I might have to start from much farther down the hill. I might have to negotiate with snowmobiles. Visiting it mid-week would help a lot with any potential traffic. At least for December I got my play day in and had it all to myself with cookies too.

January

Monday, January 13

The middle of January was wet and cold enough that the ski areas were getting daily dumps of fresh snow. The freezing level was about 1500 feet above Barclay, so the trailhead weather should be rain, not snow. I didn't trust that very much. The road to Barclay had been covered in snow in December. That corner of the valley gets so much shade that the snow might last all winter. I didn't know what I would find, but I knew that my legs ached from a nine mile run I did the day before. My legs wanted something easy so they hoped for a snow-free ride to the trailhead.

After turning off the highway, the road crosses some railroad tracks, turns back to asphalt for a bit and then becomes a proper gravel logging road. Calling it a logging road makes it sound like there were lumberjacks and sawdust hanging around. Logging was happening in the area. The highway side of Baring had the square cutouts in the forest from recent logging, but that was out of my way. Any logging along that road was either long ago or easy to overlook. I didn't have to deal with logging truck traffic, but I am sure that they were the justification for the road construction.

The overflowing pond continued to pour across the road. Little streams can cause big damage when it comes to eroding gravel roads. I was glad the Cherokee is skinny because that little patch of road was narrow when dry, and narrower when wet. The water ate the sides of the road and was digging into the roadbed. I hoped it hadn't dug too deep. I realized that someday that little stream could shut down the road by simply dislodging a pebble a minute for months on end. Then getting to the trailhead would be a long enough journey to be its own adventure. That stream crossing was fifteen hundred feet below and five miles away from the trailhead. That is a fair amount of elevation and distance to gain on foot.

Thankfully, December's snow melted and January hadn't produced enough to make up the difference. I was able to drive past the place I parked in December without finding a bit of slush on the road. Enough traffic had been through there to beat two gravelly ruts into the hardpacked snow. Between the ruts, the snow was high enough and solid enough to check the clearance of the Jeep. I listened to the undercarriage plow its way along. As long as the tires could hit gravel and had traction, I figured I could keep going.

A slight difference in altitude makes a big difference in snowpack. If the trailhead was a few hundred feet higher, the snows would have been too deep to drive through. I was happy that I got there, but not cocky enough to park it there. I didn't want to come back from my hike to find my car frozen in place. I turned around and parked farther down the hill at a bare spot under some overhanging trees.

Someone visited the trailhead since the last time I was there. I could see little glints of yellow amidst the gravel. Rifle shells were scattered around. Like at Eagle Lake, someone recently was bearing arms and forming a militia. Isn't that what the second amendment talks about? The trailhead is a lousy training ground or target range. It is small enough that a kid with a good slingshot could hit a pop can on the far side of the clearing. I don't think it is legal to shoot at game from there. If the shells were there, where did the bullets go? Were they firing off into the forest? That was a very scary notion. I like to explore, but I don't like getting shot at.

A quick check of the trail made it very clear that the skis got to stay on the car. There was enough snow on the road, but there wasn't enough on the trail. I didn't need the snowshoes either, but the snow might be deep closer to the lake, so I lashed them to my pack as a precaution. The lake was only a couple hundred feet higher, but that can make a big difference in snowpack. Uncertain weather threw the rest of my gear into the pack, so I had a daypack that weighed about as much as some people's summer overnight packs. Winter day hiking in the Cascades takes as much gear as summer expeditions in nicer climes. Well, that is only true if you carry the gear you're supposed to have for safety. I've seen nuts get by in winter in jeans and running shoes, but they are setting themselves up to need the services of Search and Rescue.

The weather cooperated, considering it was the middle of winter. El Nino might get the credit. It was in the mid forties and not raining. The trees made up for that by setting up a drip as constant as a light drizzle. Cold, clear, dry January days probably don't exist under that canopy. Even without rain, I had to wear a waterproof jacket, pants and hat. Air that cold and wet can suck the heat from a body too quickly. Hypothermia can happen without a storm in sight. I was fine as long as I stayed dry but that meant protecting myself from the plant life.

It was surprisingly bright under the trees. The light was nicely diffused by the overcast. Under the trees, a cold January day had better lighting than the deep shadows of a cloudless day in October. That helped ease any down mood brought on by the constant drizzle.

As I set out there was barely enough visibility to see Baring. A lot of the view was up for interpretation. Snow stuck to its faces, which made the mountain blend into the sky. Snow doesn't stay on vertical walls long. It wouldn't take much wind, rain or sunshine to transform the snow into an avalanche.

I thought the colors would hide until spring. Winter is usually a subtle patchwork of whites, greys, and browns with some very dark greens thrown in. Under the trees the snow was no longer the purest white, but had mellowed with a bit of melting and a patina of fallen branches and moss. That wasn't a surprise and it set a quiet tone for everything else. The plants surprised me. They weren't overwhelmed by the weather. Their colors were richer because everything was drenched. Bark wasn't only brown or grey. It had a deep character that was contrasted by the grey lichens, green mosses and fungi that clung to it. I like the way rain draws out colors. Considering Seattle's rainy reputation that is a handy thing to like. Ferns had been flattened by the snow, but where it melted off, their fronds lay in the open throwing off a deep green that was somehow bright. Some of the dead trees with exposed wood had purples and blues blended in with the browns. The brightest star was a solitary red berry that had atrocious timing, though the squirrels probably thought differently. Massive cedar logs were split open where some windstorm ripped them apart. The exposed wood was a bright amber that did a better job of catching the eye with its brilliance than any flower. Something that big and bright is hard to miss.

I had to stop to look at so much of it. Romantically that was because I stood in the midst of beauty. Realistically I stopped because I was tired and the trail was sloppy and slippery. Trying to gawk and walk at the same time was one way to slip and fall.

For me, the boardwalks were the bane of the trail. They were constructed with the best intentions. They were bad enough back in the fall, but in the winter the logs were icy too. I grimaced my way along them and worried about throwing out my back or twisting an ankle.

At least when I took breaks I was paid back with glimpses of scenery that were rare. The forest was easier to look into than during the summer. Much of the underbrush dies off in the winter. With those branches out of the way, little views into copses of trees or framed vignettes of the stream stood out. That view was hidden from most of the folks who visited in the summer.

Footprints on the trail made it obvious that the lake gets traffic even after the snows fall. At least boot prints made it harder to get lost. That wasn't much of an issue on an easy hike like Barclay. The trail was very obvious, but on other hikes footprints are sometimes the only trail signs available in winter.

Summer is usually accepted as having the most hikers that litter and mess up the forest. Unfortunately, winter gets its share. There were more rifle shells along the trail. There were also candy wrappers and beer cans. In my book, chocolate and beer do not go together. Worst of all, there was toilet paper and human excrement. I can forgive someone for crapping on the trail if they were in dire distress, but whoever did that was prepared enough to have toilet paper along. They knew what they were doing. Walking through horse manure is bad enough. Horses can't help it. Those jerks were only one step above animals. The weird and too true part of it is that they are probably proud of courageously challenging authority and getting away with it. My best hope is that they don't vote. Of course if they did, it would explain some of our politics and government. There's a level of irresponsibility there that outraged me then and does so whenever I remember it.

For a lot of people though, they only go to any lake once. There are so many places to visit in the mountains around Puget Sound that they don't have to see the same place twice. That also means they can crap in the trail and never have to see it again. Is there anything more self-centered than that? Sadly yes, but what I saw was the evidence that there is an entire league of arrogant and obnoxious people that are clueless and careless. It took a lot of effort to see past their crap and their attitudes to remind myself that everything wasn't ruined. They'd only fouled one small part of the trail. My experience would only be ruined if I let them win the fight that they didn't even know they started.

Despite the challenges along the trail, things were easier than I expected. Very little of the snow made it through the trees and the brush had fallen back, so the trail had maximum elbowroom. With the leaves gone from the slide alder, there were views of Baring that aren't available at other times of the year. The clouds were lifting but I was glad it wasn't a sunny day. The diffused lighting through the overcast made Baring look much more massive and ominous.

The shoreline changed a lot since November. The lake was full and its surface was half-frozen. A continuous sheet of ice filled the middle of the lake. There was some open water at both ends of the lake and along the shorelines but the rest was a snowy white mass. It didn't look like ice. It was more like stubborn snow. The water by the beach was getting hit with enough drops from the trees that I thought it was raining. Everything under the trees was so wet that it looked like nothing would ever dry out. The trees needed the water and the fish probably loved it. Luckily, I was wearing so many layers that when I sat on a wet log my butt was cushioned and dry.

The campsites above the beach were snow free, though some of them were filled with standing water. I didn't need one for my lunch break, but I was glad to see that they weren't hidden under sloppy snow. I wanted to come up for an overnight in the next month or two. For the price of a bit of cold and drizzle, a mid-week winter camp can provide one of the quietest and most peaceful settings that I have found. That would be possible if the weather cooperated. Drizzle isn't bad, but daylong rains cramp the experience. February sometimes gets a week or two of dry amidst the wet.

I hung around there long enough to hear one large rock fall from Baring. The rock only made one large bounce before going quiet. It landed in snow instead of bouncing off more rocks. Baring looked like one massive solid rock, but that battleship-sized crack between the summits and the talus fields below the peak demonstrated how much the mountain sheds. The mountains are young and it shows. In some places, the rocks fall often enough that the plants can't put down roots.

Except for that one large loud rock fall, the noisiest thing was the flowing water. That is typical for the Cascades. Water is everywhere and usually flowing. Incidental waterfalls draining high snowfields would be major attractions in some parts of the country. In the Cascades, most of them don't have names and many of them are never seen directly, only heard through the forest or across a valley.

My forgetfulness stopped me again. Without a watch and under an overcast, I had no idea of the time. Rather than spend hours being distracted by side trails, I spent a few more minutes sitting still. It is hard to duplicate that setting and feeling. I've never seen a garden that created such a rich arrangement of quietness and infinite detail. The setting encouraged me to sit there without moving while entertaining my eye and mind with the intricacies of tree and rock. It was relaxing to sit there and watch the patterns of intersecting ripples that were formed from water dripping off the trees. The lake was so stilled by its snowcap that a drop of water made waves that were noticeable far longer than usual. Small effects in quiet places are very noticeable. Maybe that is why I like hiking. In town, there is far too much noise and chaos for the small things to show through. I like watching the small things.

On the way back, boardwalks and tired legs slowed me down. I can't blame the folks who built the trail. The Forest Service is not known for massive budgets. They built the best they could that was safest for the land and the hikers. Besides, if all trails were designed for optimal safety to the hiker and the environment, the entire trail system would be expensive boardwalks with industrial no-skid surfaces. It would make nature too remote for me. Boots have to get muddy sometimes. Hiking at a snail's pace was not aerobic exercise though.

A bit later, I was startled into realizing how much I was wrapped up in my own head. A quiet couple suddenly appeared and I snapped awake. I was so oblivious to the world around me that when a bit of reality showed up, my mental transmission ground a few gears. They hadn't expected to meet anyone either, but once they got to the trailhead and saw my car they knew they wouldn't be alone. I stammered for a bit before becoming sociable again. It was pleasant chatting with them. They were new to the area and didn't see any reason to wait until summer to start hiking. They were a nice quiet couple. I pointed out some of the good and bad stuff up the trail and suggested some other hikes too.

Moments like that are fine measures of how a hike works on removing the mind from its normal routine. Switching from being very introspective to open and friendly was a deliberate and significant action. It wasn't a chore. I like people. Until they came along, I didn't realize how far afield my mind had wandered. Luckily, my mind and I like being in both places. I can enjoy solo hikes without a word spoken or twelve hour talkfests with a good friend on a good trail.

The remaining hurdle on the way out was the forest limbo dance. A couple of trees had fallen across the trail during one of the storms. One log was large and on the ground. The only way past it was to sit on it and swing my legs over. The other one had a two foot gap under it and was two foot in diameter. Sliding through on my belly wasn't appealing, but I tried and stopped when I found that my pack and I were larger than I thought. Taking the pack off wasn't as big a deal as realizing how much muck was down there. Hopping up on top was a bit much without a trampoline, so I gave in and detoured by trudging up the hill a bit to where I could sit and swing over. Winter hiking involves a lot of sitting on wet logs and doing laundry when I get home.

Either I hiked faster than I thought or I was becoming more familiar with the trail. Nothing else on the trail distracted me, so it was a short walk back to the car. On unfamiliar trails, I frequently think that the car is around the next corner, then the next, and so on, until I am focused on getting to the car instead of enjoying the trail. Each distraction points out how much farther I have to go. Knowing where the trailhead was allowed the time go by easier.

The skis stayed on the car and the snowshoes stayed on my pack. That was rare for a January outing. I didn't complain. For me, skis and snowshoes are simply tools to let me hike in the winter. If anything, I felt somewhat silly for carrying the snowshoes along when they weren't necessary. Ah, but for those times when they come in handy I am very glad to have them along.

Winter wasn't over and the snows wouldn't stop, so snowshoes and skis would be part of the plan for months. I wanted to check my calendar to see if I could manage an overnight in February, but all of that information was at home and that was where I was headed.

February

Monday, February 24

February was a month of extremes. That is one reason very few people hike then. In town, the weather was either clear and very cold, or warm and very wet. Warm and wet in town meant feet of snow dumping in the mountains. Barclay was in the middle. That gets very messy. As usual, I had no idea what would be waiting for me up there: snow, mud, slush or freezing rain. Despite the conditions I planned on camping overnight at Barclay, but that idea got swept aside in the chaos of everyday life. I settled for a dayhike.

It was a blue sky winter day, but a storm came through the previous weekend. That made the skiers happy. The drive that morning was gorgeous and distracting. The mountains were the whitest I had seen them in a long time. The snow was fresh and the sunrise colors were slow to fade. I pulled over a few times to sit there and look at the scenery. That much snow and that much sunshine usually don't happen close together in Washington. The clouds rarely part long enough for a view, but when they do it is a marvelous day to forget about your list of chores and fall in love with the area again. If we saw it every day it would be ignored. Covering it in clouds for most of the season makes each new sighting exciting.

The turn for Barclay was low enough that the rains washed away the snows. That left a messy road. Mud on the Jeep is a good thing. What fun is it to have an SUV and only drive it on asphalt?

The little pond, that had become a stream, continued eating the road. Someone placed traffic cones in the water marking the edges of the remaining roadbed. Outside the cones were new sudden drop-offs. That was one of those road hazards that are so small that they would never be featured in an SUV ad, but are sneaky enough to cost you lots of money and embarrassment when you have to get a tow truck to pull you out. If you can't tell, I get cautious around these little features.

Well, bummer. That driving adventure didn't last long. Less than half a mile farther was a "ROAD CLOSED" sign. Stretching behind it was a long crescent of a crack in the road. Sometime in the last month, the rains softened the streambank that bordered the road. The land slid enough to make the worst crack more than a foot deep. It ran through the middle of the lane for about four or five car lengths. Evidently, some folks didn't worry too much about it. It was possible to avoid the sign, the cracks, and the traffic cones by driving with one wheel in the opposite ditch on the hill side of the road. I parked the car on the legal side of the barrier. Going farther wasn't obviously going to buy me much. There was no way to know if there was another slide just around the corner, or if my car would be the one that opened the cracks too much. Getting my car towed out of the stream at the bottom of the hill would have been bad enough. Convincing a tow truck to sneak past a "ROAD CLOSED" sign would be ridiculous.

Just like taking weather in stride, I decided to accept the road closure and hike the road rather than turn back. Besides, walking a closed road is easy. It takes longer and I might not reach my original goal, but there'd be something to entertain me if I kept my mind and senses open.

After making sure that my car was safely out of the way, I got ready for a hike. As I was about to lock the car, a compact SUV came up the hill. The driver hoped to make it to the trailhead, but was hesitant because of the sign. All she wanted to do was take some pictures of the mountains covered with fresh snow. She liked the view from the trailhead. I didn't blame her. It was a gorgeous day. She didn't have the time to walk there though, so she maneuvered her car past the sign and drove up the hill and out of sight. To her, that photo was worth risking her car. That was obviously not a choice that I would make. I looked on the bright side. When she came back down, I could get a road report. Until then I was her backup. If anything happened, I knew where she went.

The first part of the hike surprised me by not being a normal bit of forest. There was a lot more moss. Some of the moss was so thick that it was hard to tell the difference between flat topped boulders and tree stumps. Branches and tree trunks were completely wrapped in fuzzy green. Moss grew on the north, east, west, south and tops of trees. I couldn't see the bark. The area was like a pocket of the Hoh rain forest. It is too easy to drive past natural wonders while watching for potholes and I had never paid much attention to that patch of forest while driving.

Icicles hung from the moss. It was a very cold version of the Hoh. The ground was moist and smelled fertile. Things wanted to live there. The struggle wasn't against the environment but against each other. The only reliably open ground was the road and it looked like the plants had plans for it too. Everything else was tightly packed trees or thick undergrowth.

Despite soggy surroundings, the air felt dry. It was good hiking conditions. There is about 1,500 feet of elevation gain between the highway and the trailhead, so it wasn't surprising that walking up the road kept me warm. It was a good day for a workout.

While I can enjoy abandoned roads when the trails are closed, there are some features of roadways that are too distracting. A series of power lines run through that area. Their hums and pops worried me. I've heard the scientific arguments that should calm my fears. A part of me ignores all of that when it is near something that causes the air to crackle and pop. That might not be good for me and I kept moving to get out of their neighborhood.

Away from the power lines, the forest was much noisier than I expected. Wind and water seem like they should make only innocuous background noises, but they did more than that. Wind whistled through the trees as always, but made more noises than only the movement of leaves and twigs. Falling trees can be caught and propped up by a neighbor. Every gust of wind that rubbed them together sent out a noise that sounded like a tree would fall any second. Any springtime forest hike has at least a few trees across the trail. It is not a rare event. I definitely was not comfortable with the idea of one falling in my vicinity, but the sound made me realize the stages it went through. Trees grow, but someday they fall and die, and might hit bump their neighbor on the way down before they get to rot and decompose.

Another noise stopped me. Something very rhythmic and cyclical was out of place. At one small stream hidden in some trees, the water didn't sound like the regular burbles of a cascading stream, but more like the bamboo water features in a Japanese garden. It was below me on a steep hillside where I couldn't get to it, but somehow there was something in a stream that kept filling with water and then letting it loose in a clunk and a splash. When I first heard it, I thought that some animal was coming through the trees one step every five seconds. That would make a big animal. It never got closer and didn't seem put off by me, so after a while I realized that Mom Nature was just doing some very organic hydraulic engineering.

I started to wonder about the photographer who drove past the sign. After about an hour of walking, I hadn't seen or heard any sign of her. Lots of side roads angle off into the bush, so if she was up one of those I would never know where she went. A short while later I heard her car coming down the road. When we met again she was 2.2 miles from the trailhead. It was nice of her to note that for me. According to her, the road was fine. It was snow-free until the last few hundred feet before the trailhead. She even found another truck parked there. Evidently, even large trucks were able to get by the crack without a problem.

At that point I realized that by parking legally down by the sign I maximized the risk to my car. Safely parking the car on the correct side of the sign meant it was going to sit for hours on ground that was trying to fall apart and it might get bumped by folks using the spot to turn around. Oh well, so much for being a goody-two-shoes. I continued walking up the hill.

The road made a comfortable and convenient trail. The forest was a little dark, but that was no different from the official trail. Ironically, I realized that the area along the road is wilder than the area around the trailhead. Bugs and varmints learn how to get food from people and know where to find them: at the trailhead, along the trail, and at camp. Along the road the critters see cars and trucks, not hikers and skiers. They don't learn critical begging and thieving skills. Everyone drives past them quickly, they run away, and they remain wild.

At the trailhead, the lack of snow didn't hold back the idea of winter. A wind blew down the valley and dropped the wind chill enough that I put on my heavy winter shell. Looking at mountains around me, I saw more snow up there than I thought was possible. Enormous snowbases are nothing new, but the snow was piled in places that couldn't hold it for long. Soon there would be a flock of avalanches. Even the vertical walls around Baring were plastered. The sunshine made it a too brilliant white mountain. In January, I thought it would all get knocked off. Was that snow from January or the most recent snowstorm? In either case, it would be awesome to sit at Barclay Lake and watch the avalanches fall.

I wanted to spend that time at the lake and enjoy a nice long quiet afternoon watching nature shed snow, rocks and ice in quantities large enough to smother a house. What I want to do and what I get to do are not always the same thing. The long walk to the trailhead was enough for me. The previous day had been another nine mile training run for a marathon and I didn't want to push it. The idea of using wobbly legs to walk on slippery ice-covered boardwalks seemed terrible and unsafe, or at least not worth the risk. I took some pictures, had some lunch, and turned back down the hill.

With the wind behind me, staying warm was easier and I felt more energetic. It was also easier because I was walking downhill.

On lots of Forest Service roads, there are unmarked side roads that vanish into the brush. Ignoring them is easy but my curiosity disagreed with that notion. Checking out every one is unrealistic. Some go on for miles, but I thought I had enough energy to investigate the beginnings of a few. I was most interested in the ones that snuck towards the slopes of Baring. If I wanted to follow them farther, I could come back some other month and use my mountain bike to explore their length. That was a reasonable thing to keep in mind for March. The Forest Service might wait months for the worst flooding to pass before they fixed the road.

There were probably a half dozen obvious side roads to pick from. Some of them were so overgrown that they could be mistaken for random gaps in the forest except that they were unnaturally straight. Twin ruts were the convincing evidence that people and their vehicles had been there within the last few years. Up by the trailhead, one short straight side road ended at the outlet stream: Barclay Creek. The water cut a course through a pile of rocks and was nice to look at. Standing on a rock pile there I had a nice view of Baring. It wasn't as nice as the view from Barclay Lake, but it was a shorter hike than the trail to Barclay. About halfway down the hill another road was being officially "abandoned for storage" by the Forest Service, which sounded like a fancy way of spinning a low maintenance budget. About a hundred yards in, it was being reclaimed by a stream. All the tire tracks stopped at one well-positioned three foot wide water filled pothole. The shortest and lowest road that I checked turned out to only be about fifty feet long, but it was the prettiest. It probably existed for the simple reason that someone wanted to have a campsite in the forest. There wasn't a view, but the setting was about as sylvan as is possible. A little flat spot on the side of a ravine was surrounded by trees towering and twisting overhead. Even on a very sunny day, very little light filtered through. The light came through green from all the moss in the way. It looked like a good place for mythical creatures to gather around the small fire pit that was there.

Mythical creatures may seem appropriate, but the only other animal I saw was a ruffled grouse. It was not happy to see me and scared the something out of me when it burst out of the bushes. Those birds are the noisiest fliers I have ever come across. Owls must cringe every time one flies by.

There were about a half-dozen other roads. Some led away from the mountain. Some followed the powerlines. Some looked like settings for nefarious deeds. I'd seen enough for one day.

I looked forward to seeing what happened to the main road. How long would it take to fix it? In the meantime, I could use my mountain bike to get to a trailhead. It isn't easy, but it is a way to get to trails that have no crowds. Barclay is so obviously overused on the weekends that maybe it could use a year off as the road crews fixed things. Even walking in can be fine. If everyone has to do it, that only increases the chance of having a nice quiet campsite. If all else failed I'd hike into Eagle Lake through the back door instead.

In any case, I waited for our tax dollars to fight off Mother Nature while I considered numerous alternative plans for my March trip. Oh well, that's what hiking is like in the land of the wet.

March

Monday, March 24

The road was closed in February and there was very little reason for it to be fixed. Rain can undo any road construction and the rainy season would hit the area with a lot more storms. In its first three weeks, March received twice the normal rainfall. That much water would make the crack worse. There was also that spot closer to the highway where the pond overflowed and was eating the roadbed. More rain would make that deeper and the roadbed narrower. Water eats roads quickly and there was no reason to suspect that one hadn't succeeded. The car wouldn't get me to the trailhead, so I geared up for using my mountain bike to get me there.

Despite the near record rainfall, I managed to pick a day between two storms. The clear sky brought an unseasonably cold night. There was frost in town. It was the fourth day of spring and the weather acted like it hadn't heard the news. In the Cascades, seasons show up whenever they want to. At least for my hike I had blue skies and frost, which was far better than grey clouds and pelting rain.

I had some luck. The stream at the bottom of the hill must have been too slow to do damage fast enough. It made progress on chewing into the roadbed, but the remaining gravel was wide enough and shallow enough to drive through.

The crack in the road continued to grow as the road slid down the hill. That hadn't stopped some folks from driving past the "ROAD CLOSED" sign in February. I felt a little silly parking at the sign, but you know my reasoning. In March, the problem was obvious. The road was vacating the premises. The cracks had expanded and deepened. Half of the road surface had sunk about a foot. The crack was about two to three feet deep. I didn't want to drive anywhere near that. Other folks agreed but instead of turning around or stopping they used their cars to eat into the hillside on the other side of the road. The damage from nature and drivers combined and continued.

My mountain bike and I traveled across the United States a couple of years earlier, but it had been months since I last used it for anything more than catching cobwebs in the garage. I traveled those 3,800 miles with road slicks. Knobbies were a better idea on a logging road, but I didn't have the right tires and tubes. With a freezing level below the trailhead and no butt calluses, I got ready to ride my road slicks a few miles up 1,500 vertical feet of gravel logging road. I know that the right equipment makes a big difference, and that I didn't have it, but that didn't stop me from trying.

About a hundred yards later I was hunting for my lungs. I was huffing and puffing so hard that it felt like I'd left them behind. Finding my heart was easy. It pounded away at my chest telling me to slow down. It didn't get its way. Going any slower would have meant falling over. Oh well, the important thing was to get a good workout. The road seemed steeper than when I climbed it in the car or in my hiking boots.

The breaks gave me a chance to look around. Down in that section of the woods the moss is magnificent. The trees didn't look like they needed bark. The moss covers everything up so why have bark? Rocks, trees, old stumps, and unidentifiable lumps in the forest were all simply surfaces to hold the moss. The entire forest looked soft. The forest was also very thick. The only evidence of life were the sounds it made. There was no way to see anything in there, but a few minutes into any of my frequent breaks my breathing would quiet enough for me to hear bird songs, beating wings, and woodpecker knocks. It was a very busy place, very nearby, and very hidden from sight. Nature was waking from winter.

A lot of that natural beauty was lost to me while I rode. Between watching the road for sharp rocks and glass, and listening to my body complain, I didn't get much of a chance to look up at trees and hills while I was pedaling.

As tough as it was, at least biking was faster than hiking. About an hour later, I was at the trailhead. Getting the slick road tires to grip on the packed snow near the top was a challenge. You want a moment that doesn't show up in equipment catalogs? Try maintaining balance on a mountain bike while riding uphill in freezing conditions with an overstuffed daypack strapped to your back while navigating rocks, ruts, slush and ice. Right there I deserved a doughnut. Unfortunately, my breakfast had only consisted of a banana and a cup of tea.

My grind up the hill was celebrated with extreme exhaustion when I reached the trailhead. Peeling my body from the bike seat was an ordeal. My legs and butt had committed themselves to getting the job done at all costs, which meant I had no flexibility left when I tried to stand on my wobbly legs. An entire eight hour ride on my cross country trip was not as bad as the muscle aches I had from handling bumps and avoiding road hazards while grinding up through gravel. My legs were so tired that they trembled.

It feels good to think ahead and have it work. I knew that whatever I wore would be drenched with sweat by the time I reached the trailhead. At the same time that I was hot and sweaty from pedaling, my polypro turtleneck was covered in frosty condensation. It hadn't iced over, but it wasn't going to keep me warm after the sweat cooled. I had packed an extra. The sweaty turtleneck came off, but I had to hurry. Stripping down to bare skin did an amazing job of waking me up. The occasional gust slapped me upright. Those warm dry clothes felt more luxurious than any fancy clothes I own.

Those who know me are chuckling because they know my idea of fancy clothes is clean jeans.

There wasn't much snow at the trailhead. Sometime in the last month, those rains washed it away. There was enough snow left to show tire tracks. Someone had driven up before the last storm, camped and then driven out. Snow filled their uphill tracks, but not their downhill tracks. Their adventure only extended as far as the trailhead. The remains of their campfire were in the middle of the gravel lot.

Part of what I carried on my overstuffed daypack was a pair of snowshoes. They were an insurance policy in case the snow was deeper than my shoes. Carrying skis on the bike is possible and is also a fine example of the word awkward. Snowshoes are more maneuverable in the trees, lighter than skis, and are easier to pack. I really wanted to get to the lake after what felt a bit like a failure last time. What are a few more pounds on a sweaty biker's back?

At the trailhead, I realized that the snowshoes weren't necessary. There wasn't enough snow. That saved me from the experiment of strapping snowshoes onto bike shoes. Hiking shoes made more sense but I'd run out of room in my pack and had to get by with my low top, worn down, stiff soled, touring bicycle shoes.

Hiking in biking shoes was laughable. Within the first tenth of a mile my feet got wet. Under the trees, there was more mud than snow. That wasn't the first time I was glad for thick socks. Luckily, or through experience, I have an appreciation for what is uncomfortable versus what is a danger sign. Cold, wet feet can be dangerous, but mine were merely ticked at their owner.

Any view out past the trees was mostly muted. The longer views were white with very small dots of tree and rock for contrast. Baring was still plastered. The north face was so snow covered it looked freshly whitewashed. It held snow better than I thought it could. Under the trees though, the world was turning to spring. Random spots of sunshine coming through the needles were not only green, but were also highlighted with crystals and glints from frost and dew. Catching the forest with such a mix of seasons is a rare event. I walked slowly to take it in. Of course, I didn't have a choice. Hiking through mud in biking shoes is not a recipe for speed.

My eyes loved the scenery, but my head was a little ticked at the snowballs the trees threw at me. A storm's snowfall takes days or weeks to hit the ground. It might fall a few miles through the sky within an hour, but getting those last hundred feet from the branch to the ground requires patience. The snow sits on the branches until something gets the branch to dump its load. It was sunny and under the trees it rained melted snow. The clumps of snow falling a hundred feet made me wonder if I should have kept the bike helmet on. At least none of it ran down the back of my neck.

One of the other pieces of equipment that didn't come along on the bike was my walking stick. The pragmatist in me simply picked up a fallen branch. The laundry clerk in me noticed that a stick in the woods is much messier than a ski pole. My gloves were a mess as soon as I picked up the wet and slimy thing.

Trails in the winter and early spring get even less maintenance than their approach roads. With a few storms recently passed, I wasn't surprised to find an extra tree or two across the trail. They were a few feet in diameter so my choices were crawling underneath through mud, climbing over a snow covered mossy log, or picking my way around through wet slippery underbrush. Isn't hiking in pristine conditions fun? At least the views and solitude are worth all that time in the laundry.

Bodily functions happen, so it became necessary to take a few steps off the trail and into the woods. I don't like to dwell on where I unzip, but there I stood with a nice view of a bit of a stream, some snow covered stumps, and younger trees bending under the weight of the snow. If I am going to take a break, it might as well be somewhere scenic. I didn't expect it to also be animated. Through the middle of that nice winter garden bopped an otter. I had never seen one in the wild. It was more than two feet long and shaped like slick-haired slug of furry muscle. The nature programs on television show how graceful they are underwater, but the stream there wasn't deep enough to swim in. I got to see it hopping across snow and mud. It was forced to hop along by putting a great arch into its back and the popping forward on tiny legs. It needed to take lessons from a rabbit if it wanted to travel that way. I couldn't stand there for long with my pants unzipped, but I didn't want to scare it off. There was no way I could get to my camera. Any sudden movement would have startled it. All I could do was watch it go by and wish it well. That was what amazed me. How could it miss me? I am over six feet tall and wore a huge poppy orange jacket. I couldn't hide. That was a very determined otter that wasn't in a playful mood and wasn't distracted by anything. It moved like it was very serious and determined and couldn't be troubled with acknowledging some pesky human. I wondered where they lived and if there was any hope of finding them and watching them in the water. Somehow they survive a stream that dries out. Do they head up to the lake or work down towards the valley? I didn't know.

The snow got deeper farther along the trail. Surprisingly, that made the boardwalks safer. The slippery boardwalks are terrible after a rain or with a bit of ice on them. Let a winter's dump of snow consolidate down and you end up with a good high traction surface. Well, at least it was better than smooth wet wood. The footbridge was the opposite. It usually had traction from its scattered sharp gravel surface, but that was covered. I almost slipped off because I was overconfident and let go of the handrail. Simple mistakes can make big problems miles from the nearest road.

Sun shone through as though it tried to dispel my memories of the dark forest. The eye is such a fine camera for such times. Mechanical devices have the nasty habit of including everything in view. My camera would record the scraggliest fractured trees and messy banks of mud. My mind recorded sunshine striking snow and drops of water, and then reflecting off in all directions to catch the forest's fresh bright green highlights. The dark ground served as a backdrop that framed the trees, snow and stream into an image that will stay with me. Times like that are reason enough for hiking.

From a more pedestrian point of view, it was amazing that my bike shoes were no wetter than they'd get walking through a wet parking lot. Even the mud had been less of a problem than I expected. That was all true until I got close to the lake. The slight rise in elevation near the lake meant the snow deepened. In the meantime, the spring sun made me get out the shades. The combination of fresh sunlight and deeper snow meant deeper footprints. Snow fell into my low-tops and seeped into my socks. My feet got soaked.

Most of the snow down low was melted, so I expected the lake to be melted. I was wrong. The only open water was along the beach by the campsites. The deep white ice had pulled back about twelve feet from the shore. Instead of open water lapping on the sand, there was a mottled translucent white band about four feet wide that followed the shoreline. At first, I was disillusioned because I thought there were bottle caps on it. While I was leaning forward to get a closer look, one of the trees dumped a branch-full of snow into the lake. I realized that they weren't bottle caps. They were trapped air bubbles and clumps of snow within a band of frozen slush.

When I got to the lake in the fall there was enough room on the beach to play Ping-Pong. Those days were gone. Eating lunch at the lakeshore in March meant shuffling along a three foot wide band between trees while they dropped slush-balls. Seeing the lake in the sunshine like that was memorable though. Almost all of it was a pristine white. The surrounding hills were covered with trees that were covered with fresh snow. It felt like spring because the sun was out and the evidence of winter was melting. The side of Baring facing me disagreed. It was totally in shadow and looked wintry and ominous. It looked like a grumpy cousin that frowned on its sunny relative.

The peacefulness was interrupted with a roar. I thought I heard an avalanche behind me, but looked up and saw it in front of me. It was halfway down the face of Baring. A narrow chute funneled what seemed like wisps of snow into a pile that could probably cover my house. Evidently, what I heard from behind me was its echo. Baring must be unclimbable under conditions like those. Two more avalanches fell within twenty minutes. They always fascinate me. The trick is that by the time I heard one, it was mostly finished. Baring looked close, but like lightning and thunder, the avalanche and its rumble don't get to Barclay at the same time. A thousand feet away was a one second delay, so by the time I heard it and zeroed in on the sound, the action was mostly over. I like watching them, and I was glad I wasn't closer.

By the time I turned to leave, the clouds of the next storm worked their way across the sun. The blue sky left quickly. Baring blocked some of the sunshine too. Back under the trees, it was barely above freezing. Barely above freezing is enough for more melting though, so the trip back out was wetter and muddier than the trip in. My shoes were wet enough that the water flowed through them. My feet swam in my shoes. Even the walking stick was too cold to hold until I put on a second layer of gloves.

Lighting is so important to good photos and many of the shots I didn't take on the way in were in shadow on the way out. A few times the sun came through a notch in the ridge and relit some group of trees. For the most part though I concentrated on getting my cold feet out of there.

I hoped to see the otter again, but wasn't surprised that it didn't show itself. I did see a lot more of its tracks running across and along the trail. I wonder if I was watched on the way out. If so, I hope it pardons my singing.

Back at the trailhead, the shadows and the clouds made lots of progress, but the road warmed enough to clear about half of the snow. My tire ruts had melted down to gravel. I appreciated the improved traction. Steering road slicks down an icy logging road was not something I looked forward to. Every bump and blind corner kept me from simply coasting back to the car. Big bumps used pain to convince me to slow down. Too much speed and I couldn't make the turns. I rode the brakes a lot.

If I was going so slowly, then how did I get back to the car in twenty minutes? That's almost as fast as I drove on that road. Evidently, I had more fun than I knew.

Some intrepid person with an econo car parked behind my Jeep. Most of the road doesn't require a truck or SUV, but that first stream had grown deep enough to seep past the bottom of its doors. Maybe it was a rental, or maybe it was not that deep, or maybe that was the driver's way of washing the floorboards. I didn't see anyone, so I couldn't ask. They weren't on the trail. I wondered what side road they were exploring.

I also wondered how much road would be left in April and what I would have to do to get to Barclay for a quiet overnight.

April

Tuesday, April 22

Springtime was in the lowlands. Well, at least the city forecast was for blue skies and sixty degrees. I woke up to grey skies and leftover raindrops on the skylight. Evidently, the weather changed the forecast. At least it wasn't snow.

I visit the web site of the Washington Trails Association (wta.org) before most of my hikes. It is a good source of unofficial trail reports. Volunteer reports aren't very regular or structured, but that's okay. I look for fresh updates about trail conditions and maybe learn something new about the place. That morning I hoped someone had posted a road report that said the road was fixed and open. The most recent post was mine from March. I couldn't help me much. Luckily, the official site for the Forest Service site was up to date. The news wasn't any better though.

I shoved the mountain bike into the car. Some folks ride them for the riding. For me, bikes, skis and snowshoes are simply other ways of getting somewhere. The snow equipment stayed home. The ski areas were closing because the snow was melting. They were higher than the lake, so I suspected any snow on the trail would be replaced with mud.

It is always tough picking the right clothes for a spring hike. There is no way to know if the trail's own little weather system wants to act like winter, spring or summer. The only thing I could rely on was that it wouldn't be the dry cold of autumn. Optimism won out and I packed for weather that was only slightly miserable. I guessed that the rains wouldn't be too bad and the air would almost be warm. The number of layers hadn't changed from the winter, but they were thinner and lighter which was fine by me.

At the bottom of the Forest Service road, the pond had retreated. The ditch it cut was probably too much for a sedan, but it wasn't an issue for a slow drive by an SUV. That was a big relief. It wouldn't take much more runoff for that little stream to eat the road.

The road hadn't changed. It was closed and I parked in the same spot as last month. For a moment I couldn't see the sign, but it was obvious that the road was worse. The crack had grown and tried to swallow the sign. As it got wider and deeper, it toppled the sign. I picked up the sign and set it on level ground. The road looked terrible. The chunk that had broken off was sinking and sliding down the hill. Someone had a lot of work ahead of them. If that wasn't enough, because there was less road, folks drove by the sign and the crack by digging deeper gouges in the opposite hillside. Things weren't getting better on either side of the road.

My problem was getting my butt to the trailhead. This time my bike had knobbies. Riding a gravel road in slicks was a fine pragmatic solution to do once. Better tires didn't make the hill shorter or less steep, but a bit more traction and steering control made my life easier. All of that skidding off rocks or spinning out in gravel got tiresome last time.

Climbing that hill is seasonless in some ways. Particularly, grinding out 1500 feet of elevation gain in about five miles burned so many calories and worked up such a sweat that I was warm no matter what the air temperature was. Sweat does matter when the air is below freezing or in the heat of summer, but there is a temperature band where everything balances. It was spring and I was in that zone. After only five minutes of riding uphill, I knew I didn't need a jacket.

Biking up the hill was a little faster than hiking but much harder. Most of the time saved was eaten up in getting the bike ready. Coming back would be much better though so I invested the effort in grinding my way up the road.

The ride was tough enough that it was hard to see anything besides the gravel a few feet ahead. The road was uneven enough that I couldn't play tourist. I had to continually watch and steer because of the potholes, fallen branches, gravel patches, and runoff gullies. Whenever I hit any of those, I had to be ready to straighten up and power my way through. It wasn't hard to lose my momentum and it was a pain to get started going uphill on a gravel road.

The fact that I couldn't take in the views was a non-Issue. The cloud deck was low enough that anyone unfamiliar with the area would probably guess that the sides of the valley were just low hills, not craggy mountain ridges striped with slender shoots of waterfalls.

When I glanced away from the gravel, I noticed the fresh signs of the season. The three leaves of newly sprouted trillium were out and just beginning to show signs of a white bud. Fiddleheads gave away the location of another growth of fern. Almost anything growing had small color samples of spring greens. Right then though everything looked shy and cautious as if they waited to make sure that it was safe to come out.

Spring officially starts on the equinox, but the environment picks its own timing. As the weeks go by, the signs of spring march up the mountains. Trillium might be blooming at 2,000 feet in April, but if you couldn't visit them then and there, come back later and climb a bit higher. Don't wait too long. The land only lets you climb so high.

Don't get the impression that I hopped on the bike and sweated my way up fifteen hundred feet without a break. It is embarrassing how often I stopped to give my legs, lungs, or morale a break. Stopped for one thing, I would then notice my heart hammering away. I'd wait for it to relax again. The term heartbreak means something else to most folks, but that was what I needed: a break for my heart so it wouldn't break. I guess one test of the weather was to see which happened first during a break: my heartbeat returned to normal, or my body got chilled. It must have been just right because they tended to coincide.

The trailhead was snow free. There were patches of snow beside the road, but they were like fugitives hiding from the law, though in this case the law was astronomical and was going to eventually bring the sun down on them. That wouldn't be very soon though. There was no sun to see.

Someone had childishly written, "everyone is dead", on the trail report posted at the trailhead. The ignorance of the "ROAD CLOSED" sign and such a macabre and unnecessary notice reminded me that there are a lot of odd and irresponsible people out there. My hope was that they were immature because they were young, not because they were clueless.

Like in March, my knees were wobbly when I got off the bike. The knobbies helped the ride, but they didn't make a big enough difference to keep my legs from shaking. It felt good to put on a warm and dry shirt in place of the rapidly chilling wet one. Polypro keeps a body warm when wet, but it works even better when dry.

The clouds hadn't moved. It wasn't raining, but everything was damp from fog and wandering mists. Like the trailhead, the trail was clear of snow. A little warmth went a long way towards making the hiking easier. Under the trees, it was as dark as ever. Near the trailhead are places in the forest where there is very little undergrowth. The canopy is tight enough that below is nothing but tree trunks, dead branches and fallen needles. Despite that, there were shades of green. Moss was happy in there. It covered some of the trunks as if to remind hikers that everything in the world wasn't the brown of mud and wet bark.

One stump stood beside the trail like some monument. All of its bark was gone and what remained were alternating streaks of green and brown on smooth wood. The new growth of the moss shared room with the old brown of the dead wood. I had seen the stump enough times that it acted as a guardian that reminded me of where I was and what I was about to enter.

Without snow on the trail I expected to find lots of mud, but the trail wasn't much messier than it had been in the fall. Considering that I was hiking in bike shoes, that was a relief. When I am wearing boots, I have a tendency to tromp right through shallow puddles. Low-top bicycle shoes eliminated that option and made me a more timid hiker for a day.

Moss blankets, which must have been there all winter long, looked much more alive, green and thick. A botanist would have a better guess about how many species were there. I saw at least three distinct types. One had leaves bigger than some of the neighboring bushes' leaves. It is easy to overlook moss after the big plants leaf out. The large blankets of moss draped across any place where there was room and moisture. It stood out as the greenest life in the forest.

The banes of the Cascades were budding out as well: Devil's Club and Slide Alder. The first is the worst. Bushwhacking through even small patches of it made me amazed and appreciative of established trails. Its stems are covered with thousands of small thorns that break off and become splinters by the palmful. The plant is impressive the way some cacti are hard to ignore. After it sprouts for the season, it never seems to be anything less than five feet tall with broad leaves that rival big leaf maples. Without a cleared trail through a stand of it, there is a continual battle to gingerly brush it aside while trying to look over its eye level leaves. Slide Alder isn't as bad, but I think it is much more dangerous to bushwhack through. All of its trunks are curved and covered with a slick bark. It grows in thickets were the trunks and branches intertwine and climb above head height. Getting through it requires a hiker to untangle the branches while simultaneously searching for good footing and keeping the route in mind. When it happens on a slope, it is too easy to slip and for an ankle or knee to twist. Thickets of both bordered the trail and looked like they would take over the trail at the first opportunity

Amongst the newly sprouted plants and leaves were small bushes of bare limbs that had small clumps of bright red berries at their tips. Nothing else on the plant seemed to be alive and it was amazing that something that bright would get missed by the foragers of winter. I was glad to see them because they were the one mark of color that wasn't a shade of green or brown.

The bees were ready for the next crop. Somewhere there must have been flowers because the buzzing was back. The flowers probably had some color but they were hidden.

The fallen trees continued to block the trail, which was no surprise. I didn't expect them to get cleared until after the road was repaired. Fortunately, kind people exist. One of them made life easier and cleaner by clearing some of the debris on either side of the logs. Were they the folks that wrote such bizarre things on the message board? Would I have to thank them? A couple of smaller trees had fallen too, but they were easy to step over. Climbing over the big ones was a cold and slimy experience. Wet moss isn't the most comfortable seat, but sliding across on my butt was the safest way over the hurdle.

I was pleasantly surprised that the dreaded boardwalks were not only clear of snow, but actually a little dry. For once, I was able to walk along them without fearing a slip and a fracture. That was the first time I noticed that the first boardwalk had a nice view of the stream. It is amazing how much scenery gets missed when the eyes spend their time watching for the next footstep. How many times had I walked along that bit of trail without catching the view? On a hike years ago, a friend who hadn't hiked much was amazed to find how little time he got to spend watching the scenery. Most hiking is spent looking at the ground a few feet ahead. The views only get viewed when you stop.

Another sign that spring was probably further along than I expected was that the little streams that crossed the trail were already drying up. The snowmelt from the hillsides couldn't already be done. The very rare glimpse up the hill through gaps in the clouds gave at least some view that the snowfields were only a hundred feet or so higher up. Maybe the streams gushed when the sun hit the snow full force on a hot cloudless day. That might be months later considering the shadow Baring casts.

As I crossed the footbridge, I noticed my new habit. I looked for otters. It was an unconscious activity until I asked myself what captivated me about the view. The stream is pretty enough but I spent more time on the bridge than normal. After a while, I realized my attention was bouncing around to follow any hint of a movement. My mind kept trying to make something out of hints caught or imagined of a sleek black shape darting into cover. I realized that my senses were cranked up waiting for evidence of something quickly hiding. I wanted to see the otter again. A few of the forest sounds reminded me more of an odd type of bark or yelp, but then I have a very active imagination. Maybe the otters were following the snowline up to some favorite spot. Maybe they were sitting there watching me watching for them.

The other creature I kept my senses alert for was a cougar. There are very few cougar encounters in Washington State, but the realist or the pessimist in me remembered that they are higher up the food chain than me. My best hope was that they were well fed and happy. The lack of tracks should have calmed me more than it did. That active imagination can dream up some wonders.

I didn't start out the day looking for litter. That is not why I hike. But there it was. Up a wet trail and past a "ROAD CLOSED" sign there was trash. Each hurdle shrinks the number of people that visit an area. With fewer people, there should be less pollution. That's the case in the high country. Above 5,000 feet, I rarely see candy wrappers or beer cans thrown into the bushes. In the lowlands a closed road and bad weather is not enough to stop irresponsible people. They were more resourceful and energetic than I expected. If the lake was in an official wilderness, would it make a difference to them? Probably not. Why would it? They were already breaking rules and laws. The chance that they'd get caught, charged, and fined was incredibly small. The Forest Service doesn't have enough budget to patrol the trails for litterbugs. They barely have enough resources to check on the status of the trails. Maintenance eats up budget too. Catching litterbugs is far down the list and unfortunately rightly so. If they concentrated on vandals and litterers instead of building and fixing trails there would be far fewer trails. The ones that weren't washed away or overgrown would be clean, but the network would get smaller as the other trails vanished. It is not litter that sets me to ranting. It is the attitude that some people have and my inability to talk some responsible sense into their heads.

I wasn't about to haul all the litter down on my bike, so I got a dose of guilt to go with my frustration. When I complain I like to help fix the problem; otherwise, I try to keep my mouth shut. After a harrumph and a sigh I continued.

About halfway between the footbridge and the lake there is a broad, open spot that is a streambed and probably an avalanche run. I'm guessing that snow slides are the only thing that can successfully keep such a large area clear amongst all of those large trees. That particular spot was good throughout the winter for providing the best first view of the face of Baring from the trail. Framed by pines on one side and young hardwoods on the other side, was a view across Baring's outflow and up a debris slope to a series of nearly vertical faces of the mountain. The clouds obscured almost all of that except to show a partial snowfield that started about a hundred feet above me. One cloud later, it was gone. A few seconds after that there was a peek at the next section of cliff. There was a parade of passing windows in the clouds. Seeing small pieces of the mountain through those gaps forced me to see the middle parts of the mountain. When there weren't any clouds in the way, I ignored the majority of the mountain to focus on the top quarter at the most dramatic rock. The bits I saw down low were impressive too. They simply were usually overlooked. The walls were a bit less sheer but steeper than most rock faces. Trees somehow clung to cracks and small ledges to grow taller than most office buildings, yet were hundreds or thousands of feet from the nearest flat land. How did they manage to avoid the avalanches and storm winds that cleared Baring's face? What animals were happy for incredibly safe perches? There was a lot more to Baring than simply a tall spire of rock. It had life clinging to it.

Snow covered the trail for a total of three steps. That was it for the snow at the lake. There wasn't enough for a dog to play on. Bye bye winter.

Campsites were open, though muddy, but definitely acceptable. The lake was clear of snow and even clear of waves. In the winter, covered with snow it was much quieter and the area felt hunkered down. With the ice and snow melting, all around the lake it was noisier but more peaceful. Life was relaxed and no longer defending against the extremes of winter storms. The bird song made the biggest difference. I can't identify many birds by listening to them. Claiming to identify crows and jays and other obnoxious, obvious ones is almost cheating. Knowing which shy tiny birds goes with the sweet little songs would be nice, but I heard them more often than I saw them. Sitting by the lake was a great place to hear all sorts of songs playing out around me. I guess the main messages were about fear, food and frolicking. To me they just sounded fun and numerous. The little ones must put all of their strength into each burst.

There wasn't much beach. The lake was the fullest I had seen it. With more storms to come and more snow to melt I wondered if it would get much higher or if the outflow would flood before the lakeshore was swamped. Spring floods must happen. Something uproots and drives big trees downstream. Every stream collects enormous downed trees that are piled at odd angles. Some of them are high enough above the normal summertime water level that they suggest incredibly high water in the spring. I haven't been out there while it happened and that might be safest. It would make for an awesome show though.

Because of the low clouds, the shoreline was the easiest thing to look at and it was pretty. Some of the deep greens of the pines and the browns of the forest floor are standards throughout the year. Maybe the yellow of the mossy rocks had been there too and was overlooked so easily when the mountain was within view. The bright spring greens of brand new leaves were definitely a light addition. It was a pretty shoreline and made me wonder if in Europe this would be the site of a resort rather than a bit of wild country. Either way is fine by me. I prefer the wildness, but can enjoy a good beer too.

After a bit of lunch I decided to check out the trail to Eagle Lake. I wanted to get up there again. It was not in the plans for a dayhike though. With the road closed, climbing up to Eagle after riding up to the trailhead was too much for my tired body. Besides, the views were non-existent and the top of the route was probably in snow.

I forgot what the inlet end of the lake looked like. That was where the trail to Eagle started. When I walked up there the campsites looked comfortable enough, but I wondered about the bug population. That end was acreage of marsh grass. Mosquitoes could be very happy breeding there. One defense against mosquitoes is a campsite with a stiff breeze. They can't fly fast, so a stiff breeze blows them away. The campsites at that end of the lake felt too protected from the wind. A lot of mosquitoes and no wind is a bad combination. I tried getting past the trees to check the view, but I found the shoreline before I found a view.

The rock cairn that marked the uphill trail was gone. That is an odd thing to have vanish. Did someone purposely demolish it? Maybe next time I'll rebuild it. The first hundred feet of the trail up to Eagle were in fine shape for a dotted line trail. I was tired enough to leave that climb to next time. I turned around for the day.

Knowing that I had a quick downhill ride ahead of me was surprisingly exciting. It would be more work than simply driving downhill and it would definitely be more hazardous. I looked forward to it enough that I had to continually remind myself to slowly hike back to the trailhead and take in the scenery.

Flocks of startled chickadees brought me back to the present better than any internal chiding. As I came around the corner into the avalanche chute, I startled one of their parties. They flurried into a ruckus and a panic. There were dozens of little feathered bodies within six feet of me trying to escape through the middle of a bush. It was tough on them but funny to watch. They were crammed in there and the branches were dense. They couldn't decide to jump, flitter, or fly as they tried to get through the bush without bashing each other or hitting a limb. I felt sorry for them but what could I do? I might as well enjoy the show.

After that, I slowed down a bit. Muddy trails, slippery logs and sloppy foot-wear meant that my speed probably was the same as always or maybe even slower. I felt better though. The weather was improving, so I wasn't worried about a storm coming in. I even got back in the habit of wearing a watch, so I knew I had lots of daylight left. The long days of May through August were going to be great. There'd be a lot more time to really explore the place.

Curiosity took hold at the trailhead. The idea of these trips is to explore. There is an abandoned road leading from the trailhead that I wanted to check out. The road is a slightly climbing grade that points directly at Baring. Slide alder swallowed most of it, but there was a skinny beaten path meandering up the middle. About a hundred feet in is a latrine. That's a luxury for a hiker, but the path doesn't end there. The grade continued and so did the trail. The path wasn't as well tramped down, but was obviously used. Slide alder had been hacked back by some tool-wielding human within the last year. The road couldn't go on for more than a mile without tunneling into Baring, so I knew I wouldn't have to go far to find what was up there.

It looked like any other abandoned road succumbing to nature. The land mostly stays as flat as it was built, and age doesn't add curves or straighten bends, but plants and streams cut abandoned roadbeds with roots and erosion. After a few hundred feet of wandering around bushes and stepping through running water, I found a cairn sitting in the road. Usually cairns are tiny piles of rocks that might top out at nine inches high. The rocks for that cairn were set into a crude but stable four sided pyramid that was about three feet tall. Someone had been busy. The cairn sat where the trail took a right angle turn away from the road and ran up a nearly vertical dirt trail. It looked like the kind of path we'd bash into the forest when we were kids building a tree fort. There was no attempt at switch-backs or trail building. It led up through roots and trunks along a stream and then vanished into the trees. I guessed it was the unofficial climber's approach route for getting up Baring. I wanted to climb Baring but I didn't have the time or energy for a four thousand foot climb. I was tired. Beside, I wanted to research it first to find out if there was a non-technical way up. There was no reason to start such a grunt of a climb if it required skills and gear that I had no interest in acquiring.

I switched back to going home.

There were some places I wanted to stop at on my way ride back to the car. Those great mossy trees down where I parked didn't grow at the trailhead. I wanted to get some shots of them and see if they petered out or were all around me in hiding.

My plans failed. If watching the gravel in the road was engrossing on the way up the hill, it was a white knuckle requirement on the way down. Navigating pot-holes, gravel patches, fallen branches, and washouts required all of my attention at what was probably less than fifteen miles an hour. That's because fifteen miles an hour on a bike on a busted road felt like sixty. It was a thrill and would have been perfect if I made it to the car without problems. My rear tire got flattened. The tube got punctured once by the road and once by my terrible mechanic skills. It took longer to fix the flat than it did to ride down to the car. The biggest disappointment was that I missed the shots I was interested in. The only trees I noticed were the ones lying in the road as I dodged them. I missed out on a cou-ple of pictures, but I had a blast bouncing and flying down that hill.

Down in the valley it was much warmer, but far from shorts and T-shirt weather. The plants didn't care. They were happy to be out from under the snows. In May, I guessed that the trees will be greener and the air warmer. Hope-fully the bugs wouldn't be meaner. I planned to spend a few nights camping out. It would be a long trudge in unless the road was fixed in amazingly short order. At least if the road was closed I'd have solitude. In the meantime I had to buy a spare tire and a new trail pass.

May

May 12-14

Monday, May 12

Not every hike leads to Barclay. On the way to a different hike, my wife and I dropped by the Ranger Station to renew our yearly parking pass. It is a sad fact that parking passes are now required at the Forest Service trailheads, but they need the money and the crowds are overwhelming the forests. While we were there, I got a lesson in how small contributions can have larger effects. After most of my hikes, I log onto the Washington Trails web site and post a short trail report. It's one good way for hikers to pass around the current trail conditions. The ranger recognized my name and thanked me for my reports. I was surprised that such a simple amateur report would be worth much to the Forest Service. They can't check their roads and trails as often as they would like to, so they take advantage of whatever report they can find. They especially liked the fact that I obeyed their "ROAD CLOSED" sign. We griped at each other about people driving past the sign. It was an, "Aw, shucks", moment for me when they said that they needed more people like me. The sad fact is that obeying the law is not normal. Of course, the folks driving around the sign made the road repair job bigger so more of our taxes got spent than was necessary, but too few people think that through. We Americans pride ourselves on our freedoms and sometimes extend that to ignoring laws that are inconvenient at our expense. At least that doesn't happen at the highest levels of government.

There was some very good news for me. The road was scheduled to re-open on May 8th.

My plan for May was to finally spend a couple of nights at Barclay. I like to hike in that gap between after the snowmelt and before school lets out. Of course for some lakes higher up, the snow may not melt until after school starts again. Barclay is low enough that there was a chance for me to get in there and enjoy it in solitude without freezing my butt off. My biggest worry was bugs. Each lake has its bug season and I didn't know Barclay's.

When I drove up that morning, there were lots of unknowns. That is typical of any hike. Was the road work completed on schedule? Did the stream below it wash out the other section of the road? If I wanted to get to Eagle Lake, did I need galoshes for mud, snowshoes for hardpack, crampons for the climb, or skis for the ridge above the lake? The decision about which of those toys to play with could wait until I saw where I got to park. If I parked at the trailhead, I could use the car for storage and hike back out to it for anything I needed. If I had to park at the bottom of the hill, the choice would be simpler. I'd take the snowshoes and leave the skis and crampons. The snowshoes are more versatile and are much easier to carry than skis. They are lighter than the crampons or skis, have some teeth to them like crampons, and spread my weight out like skis. They are a nice compromise.

The Forest Service erected a "Dips" sign beside the gouge left by the overflowed pond. The dip was dry which made life easier. Less than a half mile later, I saw the familiar sawhorses in the road. For a second I thought they had fixed the road but kept up the "ROAD CLOSED" sign. I didn't want the aggravation of parking at the bottom of the hill because someone forgot to take the sign home with them. Following the law can be such a pain sometimes. As I got closer, I noticed that the sawhorses were not on the road. They were beside it and the sign was gone. I could drive to the trailhead!

I smiled like it was Christmas morning. One hundred and seventy horses under my hood drove me up the hill. I looked at the road and the scenery and it was new again. I breezed past it all on the October trip, and then I hiked, biked and skied it through the winter, which gave me a completely different point of view. Bouncing uphill at thirty miles an hour was fun. I didn't have to sweat and I got to watch newly familiar landmarks flow by. I was giddy with speed. There was a bit of a mental sigh as I realized I was speeding past the heavy moss forests and missing the sounds and aromas of the woods, but I wasn't going to stop. Driving up that hill was luxurious after grunting my way uphill enough times. I grinned and loved letting the car do the work.

The trailhead was empty. Maybe word about the road re-opening hadn't gotten out. Actually, I am sure that very few people check those things in advance. Most folks get hikes in as they can, not through stints of great research for current road and trail conditions. A day opens up on their calendar and they go for it. I've done the same thing. Sometimes it is enough to celebrate the simple victory of getting out the door and away from chores. Good weather and a parking spot at the trailhead were bonuses.

The weather forecast was for two days of nice skies followed by two days of cold rain. I had enough food for at least four days and the right gear for everything up to six inches of snow and down to twenty degrees at night. Hiking the Cascades has taught me to pack for more than the plan. Storms, chipmunks and helping others happens, so I carry foul weather gear, hang my food, and carry emergency supplies. The snowline drives many of the gear choices but was hidden. The clouds obscured everything except the valley. Despite the forecast for clear skies, microclimates happen and that one around Barclay likes clouds.

My last overnight was back in the fall. That meant that I spent hours rummaging around the house and in the car looking for all of my equipment. The first overnight of the year is always like that: a bit disorganized, packed for every contingency, and undoubtedly forgetting something.

The clouds looked like they were desperately holding on to winter, but the flowers and fresh leaves on the trees were running full speed into spring. The fresh yellow-green leaves of the alders met overhead like a cathedral of white bark walls with a fresh green ceiling. Along the trail, three leafed trillium were out with big white blossoms that were even more noticeable because of the diffuse lighting. When it is bright out, the trillium are harder to spot because they like the shadows that were easy to overlook. Ferns were no more than a few small fiddleheads, but they would soon fill out into waist high shrubs. All was not glory and light though. Devil's Club shot up in stems that produced thorns now and leaves later.

Amazingly, the trail was dry. The downed tree trunks weren't slimy and the boardwalk didn't even try to slip me into the thorny bushes and mud. I was very glad for the traction, especially considering that I was carrying a pack that weighed at least fifty pounds.

I hiked quickly. Driving to the trailhead meant I was full of energy when I hit the trail. Taking pictures was the only thing that slowed me down. By 11AM, I was at the lake and picking a campsite. I felt like I missed something. I missed the grind and the exhaustion of most of my overnight hikes. Too many of the aggressive hikes I've been on involve hiking all day and falling into camp near dusk. Getting to camp before lunch was decadent. I liked it. No wonder some folks skip the long hikes. I had solitude and plenty of energy. That was a rare combination for me. I decided to take the opportunity to find the best site instead of collapsing into the first bare patch of ground.

Camp was set up less than an hour later. It was large, flat, beside the water, and had a view of Baring. In the summer it would have absolutely no privacy because it was right beside the trail. I had the lake to myself and didn't have to worry about folks peeking into my tent.

I wondered what to do with the rest of the day. In a scene straight from kindergarten, I had lunch and took a nap.

An early start, my nap, and a snack gave me enough time and energy to check out the trail to Eagle Lake and the valley floor below it: Paradise Meadow. Roaming around up there for the next couple of days sounded interesting. If the snow was good enough I would go back to the car, switch boots, and grab my ski equipment for a run down the ridge above Eagle. That sounded fun. It was very likely though that the trail was too hidden by snow. Of course in that case, spending some quiet time down by Barclay was a much more relaxing backup plan.

I didn't have a fanny pack, so I emptied my backpack and reloaded it with the snowshoes and enough gear for an emergency bivouac. In April, the cairns leading to Eagle were gone. Someone had been there since then. The beginnings of a new cairn marked the trail. There is always someone getting there first. The Pacific Northwest has some amazing people tramping around it. No matter the season or the destination, someone has been there recently. I added a stone and began the climb. The route to Eagle is an official trail, but it is a dotted line on the map and acted like it. The trail wasn't a continuous path through the forest, but was more like a series of boot paths interrupted by fallen trees, mats of needles, and small streams.

The cairns weren't the only tail markers. Strips of plastic fabric were tied to tree branches along the way. Maybe at one time, or for someone with better eyesight than me, the cairns and the strips made the route obvious. Within the first five hundred feet of elevation gain I saw at least one set of cairns, more than two colors of strips, and crossed long stretches where there was no sign except for what I hoped were boot prints. The orange and pink strips turned out to be two different routes, not just faded versions of each other. Twice I got lost when the trail got too faint to follow. Once a fallen tree obliterated any trace of where I should go. I can't even remember how I found the trail again, but I know that it involved slowly working my way back to signs like boot prints, worn logs and cut down trees and starting over again. It was hard work and I had no desire to get too tired or too lost. That is a bad combination, especially for a solo hiker.

As I climbed, the clouds lifted. I saw that I was above the snow that hid in Baring's shadow. The snow on my side had melted recently. I walked past last year's dead ferns that were a mat across the rock fields. A few of the bravest of flowers poked through, but most of the softer plants were flattened from the snowpack.

The climb to Eagle Lake is about fifteen hundred vertical feet in about a mile and a half. It wasn't until I crossed a rock field at twelve hundred feet above Barclay that I came across patches of snow. A hundred yards later, I had trouble finding dirt. Under the trees, and with that little bit of elevation gain, the snow hadn't melted enough to expose the trail. It dominated the scenery. The snowline was that abrupt. Within a few hundred feet, I passed from spring back into winter.

I found a set of old footprints in the snow. Their route didn't follow the trail exactly. That was okay. The trail that makes sense in the summer is not always the route to take in the winter. Snow smoothes over broken land. Following switchbacks becomes a silly exercise. On snow it is far easier to pick a route and head straight at it, than trying to follow every twist in a trail. The route across the snow changes as the snow melts. Those folks picked a route across rocks and streams that worked for them, but their boot prints melted through. Some of the snow bridges they used had opened into ankle twisting holes. A few years back I unofficially got involved in a Search and Rescue operation because some stranger's misstep broke his ankle as it poked through a weak snow bridge. We were on a dayhike and happened to be in the area. All we did was help carry out a couple of packs. The official response involved dozens of folks and a helicopter to get him out. The size of the response left me with the impression that I never want to be the cause of all that disruption. Rather than tempt the same fate I put on my snowshoes. They would spread out my weight and hopefully straddle any surprise holes.

It is a pity that it is necessary to spend so much attention on where your next step goes. The pocket of forest I went through was a ravine wide enough to have a snow covered pond, exposed hillsides covered with snow, and a stream winding its way towards the drop into Barclay. It was a quiet pocket of the forest that was a worthy destination, but is overlooked because it was between two more impressive spots. The season's change is most dramatic when the days get longer and where the snow quickly melts. It was happening then and there. Unfortunately, I couldn't concentrate on that. I had to watch my footsteps.

Getting myself through with the snowshoes wasn't easy. Snowshoes like snow, but I was trying to follow a trail that was very mixed up. It was mostly snow, but that was also over tree roots, across streambeds and over fallen trees. Within a quarter mile, I took the snowshoes on and off a few times. I put them on as a defense against postholing and took them off when I thought they might slip on wet tree roots or slick rocks. Progress was slow.

At the top of the gap, I saw a great sweep of uninterrupted snow. I was in the valley that holds Eagle Lake: Paradise Meadow. When I first came into the valley last fall it was a beautiful mess of mud and streams. Then, getting to the lake was an exercise in muddy maze navigation. With it covered in snow I was able to aim straight at the lake. Enough snow melted to open the streams to the air, but enough snow bridges remained to let me by. The drop into the streams was three feet deeper because of the snow piled on the banks. It would take a lot of work to crawl out if I fell in.

The clouds weren't gone, but they were above the ridge tops and I could see all the way back down the valley. I looked up at the ridges around Eagle Lake to check out the skiing possibilities. I hadn't realized how steep the land was. There was a lot of exposed rock. Whatever snow hit the steep rocks had shed in avalanches. There were some routes there, but I am not an expert enough skier for land like that and I want to live a long healthy life. Skiing was out of the question. I had no need for the bragging rights.

Eagle Lake was almost completely covered with ice and snow. A small area near the outlet was melted and about a dozen pockets of pale blue melt water had formed on the lake's cap. Mountain lakes thaw from the edges so the ice is thinnest there. Without a distinct shoreline I didn't know if I was standing over land or lake. I hung out near the trees.

At a glance, the lake looked pristine. That was a lot of white to look at. The longer I looked at it though, the wilder it became. Avalanche debris sat on the lake's cap. Piles of snow, boulders and broken bits of massive trees sat a hundred feet out onto the lake. I guessed the snowcap under the debris was fairly thick, but I also knew the edges were melting. Half of the roof of the cabin wore a cap that was about three feet thick. I wondered if the cabin was completely buried during the winter. The idea of going around the lake was nixed. Every route crossed avalanche chutes and I preferred to see them from a safe distance. I decided to hang out by the cabin and enjoy the view where it was safe.

It was nice being camped less than three miles away. That's one of the gifts an overnight camper receives: a lot more daylight to roam around in. On a dayhike, I had to worry about getting back to the trailhead. By camping overnight I had an extra hour of daylight to play with because all I had to do was get back to camp. I didn't have to worry about avoiding traffic jams on the drive home. That extra time is when the good lighting fills the views with deeper colors. Closer to dusk it is easier to see wildlife emerge for the evening foraging. An extra hour closer to dusk makes a big difference in knowing a place's wildness and its beauty. I know I miss that on a dayhike. I treasure that when I camp overnight. Few people get to see true wilderness and a self-selected few get to see the wildness and beauty amplified as the sun goes down.

My turn around time was later than usual, but all I had to do was follow my tracks back down the hill. That's the other nice thing about snow hiking; finding your way home is much easier because you can follow your own footsteps.

I wasn't going to get lost above the snowline and below it I couldn't stray too far. Those cairns and colored strips were confusing, but on that side of the hill I was bounded by the ridge above, the lake below, and the outlet from Stone Lake to my left. That gave me a bit more confidence that following yet another set of plastic flags couldn't go too wrong. Besides, I was there to explore. I am glad I took the chance. The route down didn't cross any downed logs and it seemed to be in much better shape than my uphill route. I planned to take the route nearest the stream next time.

Back down at Barclay I was surprised and pleased to find that no one else was there. I had the lake to myself. It was a bit late, so I immediately got busy pumping water and making dinner. The trip to Eagle gave me a feeling of accomplishment and a sense of satisfaction. I liked knowing what was happening in the valley above me. At camp, the weather cleared and the bugs weren't much of a nuisance, so it looked like I picked a fine time for my visit.

I expected the night to come on slowly and undramatically. The valley walls are steep and there was a chance I wouldn't see the sun again until late morning. It was getting closer to the solstice though and the sunset had traveled far enough north of west that for a few minutes the sun shone right up the lake. A few clouds got in the way to soften the light show, which made it very peaceful. As the sun dropped to just above the horizon, the angle of light was so low that it passed under the clouds and reflected off the lake's surface to shine up into the trees. The low branches hanging over the water were brilliantly lit from below with light that danced as the small waves on the lake threw flashes onto the needles and bark. I loved it and sat there watching another rare moment of beauty. It could only happen when the sun sat above that part of the horizon and there was a hole in the clouds. That was marvelous.

Twilight in camp after dinner is a time for choosing from quiet ways to end the day. With the failing light there are precious choices to make, because there is too little time to do them all. The wind has died, so the mosquitoes freely fly through the still air. Aside from their buzzing, it is the quietest time of the day. Maybe simply sitting, breathing, digesting and enjoying the peace is perfection. The colors deepen as the sun cuts through more of the atmosphere. There's usually less light to work with, but there's more to please the eye and camera. Instead of sitting still, maybe it is time to wander around taking pictures. If the clouds are kind, the atmosphere's full palette is painted on tomorrow's weather. It takes time to fully appreciate the colors and hues and how they softly shift until after past sunset. The most intense colors are frequently on the last tip of some peak that is otherwise completely in shadow. A snapshot viewed days later shows a dark mountain with a dot of light, but the mind saw a massive richness in that color that overwhelmed everything else in view. It's the last chance to read without a headlamp for the next several hours. That's especially precious if the book is a thriller that is best not read in the dark. If there are friends around it is a good time to talk about the day and plan for the next.

All of this assumes that the campers are done with their chores. Dinner is made and cleaned up. Gear is prepped for the night. Water is stored, batteries replaced, and teeth brushed. Those who light campfires or challenge the night with brilliant lanterns aren't limited by the end of the day. They may not appreciate it as much either. Looking at the stars or listening to the birds is much easier in the dark. For me, it is the time to write. My mind is calmest because the world is quiet and my belly is full. I can write into deep dusk without a light because my hand only needs to stay inside the lines. Reading what I wrote comes much later. Sunset and darkness come much sooner than my bed time. My habits instilled at home aren't changed for a couple of nights in a tent. As glorious as sleeping ten hours from dusk to dawn might sound, reality is that inevitably the light failed before the brain was finished. The headlamp will come out to help finish the day. Usually some task is remembered late and a bit of stumbling about gets it done. After that brief bit of energy, life settles in to get comfortable and listen to the insects, birds, and flowing water ushering in the night. A bit more reading, the eyelids droop, and it's time to sleep. Maybe at sunset tomorrow I'll sit and watch. Maybe not, but that's tomorrow. Amidst the peacefulness, Baring began spring cleaning. Every few minutes, boulders broke loose and fell hundreds and thousands of feet down its face. Between the sunset and that ruckus, it was like listening to a sweet string section when the percussionist trips and hits the cymbals. The night was even more dramatic. One rockfall obviously carried dozens of rocks down into each other. Instead of a short crack I heard rumbling for long enough that I waited for something to hit the water. Twenty minutes later, I heard another and started to time it. After I found my watch, it went on for 50 more seconds. Within the hour, there was another one that went on for 80 seconds. It would have been amazing to watch, but in the dark and in my tent all I could do was listen. The lake was formed by a rockslide and I wondered if I would get to experience and survive such a major slide. Eventually the mountain quieted down and only threw down a boulder every hour or so after that.

Tuesday, May 13

I had great excuses for sleeping in. When it's in the thirties at night and the tent won't see the sun until late morning, it is easy to hide in a toasty sleeping bag. I didn't want to get up until the sunshine got past the ridge and warmed the tent.

Sunrise came late to the lake. Northeast of the lake is the ridge that tops out at six thousand feet: thirty five hundred feet above Barclay. Down by the lake the trees are enormous and close. When the sun finally got past the geology, the botany got in the way. Trees blocked the light for at least another hour. Sleeping in while warm, cozy and contented was wonderful. It was a decadent way to start the day. Alas, my bladder only let me hide out so long. Once out, climbing back in is never the same. At least when I finally got out of the tent the world was bright enough to convince me to stay up. I was in shadow and chilly, but the opposite side of the lake and all of Baring was lit up like a summer day. I stomped around wearing things like a turtleneck and gloves while waiting for my oatmeal to cook. I looked at summer and stood in winter.

Overnight the weather improved. The clouds dissipated and the wind was blessedly calm.

I decided to investigate around the lake. Most lakes have fishermen's trails circumnavigating them. They aren't efficient paths, or even stable, and make way too many detours to the waterline, but they are frequently the only way to get around a lake. Besides Eagle, Barclay also has two other neighbors about a mile or two away and a thousand feet up in another valley. They were probably below the snow level, so I thought they'd be interesting and worth some effort.

I began by hiking clockwise around the lake. That was the easy route because I knew there was a trail there. At the last campsite up by the inlet, I poked my nose into each gap in the trees looking for a route to those other lakes. When toilets are in doubt, lots of campsites sprout spurious little trails heading off into the bushes. That meant occasionally stumbling along short trails that ended in nasty litter.

I was lucky. One time, instead of litter, I found a boot-beaten track that was marked with yellow ribbons. It looked promising. It had that combination of enough traffic to beat a bit of a path and markers that showed that someone thought the route was worth a bit of effort. Unfortunately, I also found lots of downed trees blocking my path. Maybe I lost the trail after climbing over one of the logs. The beaten earth became less obvious and the undergrowth became much thicker. The downed trees and the fresh undergrowth made the forest floor very confusing. Getting over and around the living and dead plant life was not easy.

Within a few hundred feet I was stuck. Lots of fallen trees and high spring water made it hard to believe there was ever a trail there, but the markers hung from various branches as if it was the way to go. The prudent side of me realized that if I had a hard time finding and following the route, any rescue party would be days searching if something dire happened to me. If the streams weren't so full it might have been easy enough to hike up them, but I was there during the wrong season.

That little excursion was unsuccessful, but it managed to warm me up. I was back in camp before lunch and decided to take a short break before trying to get around the lake from the other direction: counter-clockwise and across the outlet. Somewhere in some sunny meadow it was probably warm enough to lie in the sun. Down in the shadows by the lake, I hoarded the heat I had generated by draping the sleeping bag over me. The nap that happened wasn't a big surprise. I woke up in time for lunch.

The first visitors arrived while I sat there eating my sandwich. A couple picked a spot on another beach about a hundred feet away past a small grove of trees. Lake acoustics are amazing. Whispers carry far. The best proof and the worst cases are parents screaming at children. When some folks are in the mood to scream at their kids, they don't care who hears it. I think they shout because shouting makes them feel better, even if it doesn't do any good. Luckily, this young woman's very nice, soft-spoken and conversational voice carried well across the water. Maybe talking to me was better than talking to her date. I never heard a word from him. She knew a lot about the area and was more adventurous than me. She'd climbed Baring years ago and confirmed that the very large cairn I found in April does mark the beginning of the climbers' route. I was surprised to hear that it does not require ropes and such, but a calm head, strong legs and the desire to not do something stupid. The route has a fair amount of exposure, which is another way of saying there are easy opportunities to fall to your death. I wanted to climb Baring but not during rock fall season so I had to wait a few months.

Before lunch was over, a group of six women hiked by. They made the biggest crowd that I had seen there. My first thought was that it must be warmer in town because they wore shorts and short sleeved shirts. I sat in my shaded camp wearing a jacket and hat as I tried to stay warm. They acted like they were headed to a day at the beach. That's what they did. They sat down on the only spot of sunny beach. It was on the other side of a tree and I hadn't noticed it. I have to get out of camp more often.

I walked to the outlet while they soaked up some sun. Crossing the outlets of lakes in the Cascades almost always involves hopping and balancing across a chaotic pile of floating logs. Slipping between them would be like falling between the wringers in an old washing machine, but massively worse. The logs move with the wind, waves and lake level, so the path changes throughout the season. It is not always clear how to get to the other side. I hoped there was a trail over there, but I didn't see one. For a lake that gets so much traffic during the peak season, I expected to see a maze of beaten dirt on both sides of the lake. My hope was that it existed and that it would be obvious after I climbed across.

When I finally got over there I found an unbroken mat of thick rain forest style moss. It covered a rock fall that butted against Baring. Under the moss and on top of the rocks were hidden fallen trees that were decaying. The area looked nice and softly green, but it was a dangerous mess to walk over. There was no trail and there wasn't even much dirt. The only places to put my feet were the moss, rocks, and dead trees. Some of the moss that looked solid spanned gaps that dropped through into three feet of darkness. Bushwhacking through terrain like that is nothing new, but it is not easy. I gave it a good shot and probably climbed a hundred feet or so above the lake. That gave me a great view back up the valley.

That climb also showed me that the bushwhacking was not going to be a fair fight. Where enough dirt collected for plants to grow it sprouted shrubbery with thorns. The climb also took me closer to the wall of rock that spewed boulders the night before. The rocks I stood on were the size of washing machines. It seemed that I'd either drop a leg down a hole or have a rock pummel me from a thousand feet up. I didn't need to get around the lake that badly. I surrendered and decided to spend the afternoon reading a book.

That view of the lake helped me understand the place better, so the trip wasn't a loss. The lake is much longer than it is broad. The side with the campsites had a soft shore. It was a long line of beach and brush with overhanging trees. There were none of those cliffs that plunged into deep pools that so magnificently blockade the shore at some of the lakes in the high country. Barclay was less dramatic and much more approachable, well at least on that side of the lake it was more approachable. The Baring side was inhospitable.

Before I got back to my tent, I met the gang of six on the trail. They were leaving but stopped to chat for a bit. One of them was nice enough to remember that she had seen someone with a big grin who claimed to have caught a long string of fish at the upper lake. That was great news. I thanked them for the information. It confirmed my notion that there was a way up there. A few minutes later they were gone and I mentally kicked myself. I missed out on some key questions. When did she meet the guy? Was it a few hours ago or last year? Which of the three other lakes was he talking about? Was it Stone Lake, Grotto, or some small hidden pond? Did she believe him? Bummer. My enthusiasm is fun, but it sometimes races me right past the best parts.

The rest of the day was one of the most peaceful times I have spent backpacking. Everyone was gone. The lake was mine. The air was warm and still. I had a good mindless book and a comfortable place to sit. It was marvelous. Hours spent like that are far better than any time I have spent in a fancy hotel. An occasional quarter ton rock bounced down Baring to keep things from getting dull. That bit of heaven lasted until suppertime.

There is something about us humans where we are far better at describing our adventures and hazards than we are at describing contentment and serenity. Maybe that explains the media's obsession and our appetite for bad and sensational news. It is easy to spend an hour describing a five minute mishap but describing those fine hours spent at the lake is much more difficult. They passed so quietly and softly that I can't remember specific things that happened but can only vaguely recall a feeling of great relaxed comfort and a desire that it wouldn't stop. A tape recorder wouldn't catch anything. A still camera captures the image better than any movie camera. I think book lovers can understand the feeling best. It is that immersion into a timeless experience where the day goes by uninterrupted as it flows smoothly along. I hope to remember that bit of peace as much as I remember my best adventures.

Eventually I got hungry. When it was time for dinner it was also time for the weather to change. The sunshine thinned as high clouds very slowly drifted in front of it. The streaks of sunlight coming through the trees and glancing off the lake faded while my dinner water boiled. The temperature dropped and the wind rose. I put on my gloves. I watched the lake from the wind shelter of one of the larger trees. After dinner, the feeling around the lake was gloomy. Choppy waves replaced the quiet smooth surface. It wasn't even dark when I decided to get back into the tent. I pulled my sleeping bag over me and read until the batteries died.

The mountains are amazing to visit because they change so dramatically. That night when I got up for a bladder break, the sky was clear and the night was bright because the moon was one day before full. It wasn't gloomy anymore. The weather forecast had been for a system to come in. I didn't believe it passed through at dusk, but I considered the possibility. A clear sky at midnight was a relief and showed hope for the following day.

Wednesday, May 14

Outguessing mountain weather is harder than making money at Vegas. The clear skies at midnight became a heavy overcast after dawn after the quickest glimpses of sunshine.

I had enough food to stay for days and good enough gear to weather a winter storm. Overpacking has its benefits. It gave me options. I thought through the situation. Going high by climbing up to Eagle wouldn't be good. Rain on snow with bad visibility did not sound appealing. Staying low was limited to hiding in the tent because I gave up on circumnavigating the lake. I wanted to stay though and wasn't certain the weather would get bad. Maybe the day would stay cloudy but dry and I could sit on the shore and read some more. I hedged my bets. After breakfast I broke camp, or at least packed up the small stuff like cook kits, food, and spare clothes. If the weather swung nice, I could stay another night. It wouldn't take much to unpack those few items. I waited on the weather by settling into the next book.

No one came by that morning. The few gaps in the clouds stitched together and the mountaintops were gone. Sometimes I chastise myself for overreacting on the side of safety. It does make me more sensitive to the environment around me though. Two chapters later, the air felt heavier. Without any kind of a rush, I put everything into my pack and got ready to leave. Before I put the pack on, I started to write a note to myself about how easily I am spooked out of camp by weather. That's when the first raindrop hit the back of my hand.

It would be a better story to say that the clouds burst forth with a downpour of rain and that I rushed for the car. That possibility was in my mind. Reality was much simpler. The rain wasn't very heavy and I took my time hiking out. When I got into the car, I needed the windshield wipers. Back home I checked the weather radar and it showed mostly clear skies except for one blob of water washing the area around Barclay. I was glad I got out when I did.

It was nice to spend a couple of nights up there and I wanted to go back for more, but it was also nice to get home and not have to worry about pumping and filtering water, getting a stove lit, or digging a latrine. The luxuries of civilization are never so apparent to me until I've lived without them for a while.

June

Saturday, June 7

For once, it wasn't a solo hike. It involved walking but it wasn't a hike at all. I learned that Washington Trails Association was going to work on the trail to Barclay. Their trail advocacy is a nice balance of lobbying and trail maintenance. It was obvious that I should volunteer and help them keep the trail in good condition. A long time ago I assumed that the Forest Service did all of the work on the trails, but I've learned that there is a somewhat organized collection of government agencies and volunteer organizations that help as they can. No one's budget is big enough. I've even seen some folks doing their court mandated community service by clearing brush from a trail.

Bushwhacking through Devil's Club once was enough to make me appreciate a good brush-free trail. It is easy to ignore the effort required to keep a good trail open and easy to walk on. My trips up to Eagle Lake made it obvious that Mother Nature never stops her attempts to reclaim those strips of primitive civilization that we cut through her wilderness. Without regular hacking, slashing, digging and filling, the trail would disappear beneath growth and downed trees or get swept away by erosion or rockfalls.

I screwed up my back years ago. I had too much fun one month and have paid for it many times since then. That makes me reluctant to sign up for chores that involve heavy lifting. Between caution and strengthening, my back had gotten back to the point that I can carry a full pack as long as I wasn't silly about it. Some biochemist's work inventing ibuprofen definitely helped. I thought I might finally be useful enough to pay back some of the benefits I have received from others' trail work without messing up my back. The responsible side of me only wanted to volunteer if I could do good work. A newer, more mature, and more relaxed side of me kept reminding me that volunteering is free labor and that they would be happy with whatever they got as long as I didn't hurt anyone or get in the way.

I was a rookie, so I read the primer listed on their web site. There was a lot of common sense safety information and advice on clothing and gear. Forget the lightweight high tech fibers; old heavy cotton has its place when work is involved. High tech clothes look great in the recreation catalogs, but work clothes can take more abuse and are cheaper. It made me realize that the high tech clothes are meant to be in the outdoors, but not in contact with it. They don't work well when they get dirty and they cost too much to risk. The WTA said that they would provide the tools and that my main task was to show up. Hiking in heavy duck-cloth bib overalls would be a new experience.

They recommended carpooling. Otherwise, all of our cars would swamp the parking lot. Carpooling only works as fast as the latest arrival, so we were a little late. Getting to the trailhead late meant less than it would for a normal job. Volunteers don't have to punch a time clock and working on Forest Service land meant there was paperwork and procedural stuff for the organizers to get through. That slowed things down enough that we didn't miss anything.

The crowd was a good mix with both genders, various ages, and a range of experience levels. I liked that. That meant there were more stories to hear. We had to wear hardhats for bureaucratic and pragmatic reasons. Our leaders for the day took the time to tell us the rules and de-stress some folks by emphasizing that safety and fun were more important than completing epic marvels of trail construction. The Trail Boss who pulled the group together wears a blue hat. Anyone with five work parties in their history gets a regular green hat with their name on it. I can't remember what the orange hat was for, but one of the experienced trail leaders had one with her name and "The Menace" printed on it. Most of us simply picked from a pile of one-size-fits-all green hardhats.

There was an obligatory safety lecture that was common sense, but a lot of common sense is not obvious until someone teaches it to you. I spent not much, but enough, time in a steel mill and around an oil depot that a lot of safety stuff is drilled into me. I didn't mind having it drilled anew. Beside the issues of the work hats and the regular hiker's outdoors hazards, the work leaders took us through the tools and their proper handling. The only tool we could bring along from home was a small folding pruning saw and a handheld pruner. They provided everything else. It was obvious why they wanted us to use the equipment they provided. Shovels, hoes, and other stuff were all Forest Service issue and had mutated from their suburban counterparts so they were better for fighting forest fires. The shovel, which has some other funky name, has more of an angle to the head and sharpened side edges so it can cut through brush and sweep aside dirt. The Pulaski is a marriage of an ax and an adz and is heavy. All the tools were heavier than what most folks have at home. The hoe was enormous. Its head was more like a dinner plate than a dessert plate. The lopper didn't look different, but the rake only had six massive teeth and was introduced as "six sucking chest wounds waiting to happen".

From there, the rest of the day was very freeform and much less structured. The trail wasn't in awful shape. Some Forest Service folks cleared the worst stuff a few weeks back, so we were instructed to work on maintenance more than repair. In other words, go out there and see what needs to be done. So much for the defined statements of work I remembered from office life. We sorted ourselves into three groups. My group was assigned the stretch farthest in by the lake. It was the most picturesque locale, but it also meant we had to carry our tools the farthest. Everyone had to carry one in each hand and you hoped you picked the tool you'd need for the task you'd find. Just because there is a lopper in your hand does not mean you'll work on trimming wayward branches. I grabbed a Pulaski and a shovel. That way if the tool didn't match the job at least I'd have heavy tools for a light job instead of light tools for a heavy job. It wasn't great logic but it was worth a shot.

We marched off into the woods, but the back third dropped off within the first quarter mile. They started to work the section just in from the trailhead. There was a bit of conversation as folks became acquainted, but carrying heavy sharp tools while hiking makes it tough to turn around and talk to someone. You didn't want to swing around and krang someone with a shovel. The tools even made it tough sweeping spider webs from my face or scratching my nose. I was glad we were on a flat trail. Those trails that gain a thousand feet every mile for hours must be ugly grunts with tools in hand.

The trail report on the trailhead board looked great. There weren't many bugs and the flowers were out. I didn't get to see much except my feet, a bit of the trail and the tool handles of the guy in front of me. Those handles were my main concern. I had no desire to wear any of the Forest Services' implements internally.

Because I was a rookie trail worker, our group leader was nice enough to find me a mentor for the morning so I could get an idea of what we would actually do. I understood getting logs out of the way, but we weren't going to do that. Instead, we started by beating back the bushes. In some sections the bushes threatened to narrow the path to a thorn bordered alley only wide enough for a dog. Did we have the right tools? Well, almost. The sharp edges of the shovel are supposed to work on stuff like that. There is a tool designed for what we did called a brush whip, but they forgot to get any for us. So we started whacking weeds with shovels. Picture it anyway you want. I tried flinging that thing around lots of different ways before I settled on my own style. What ended up working for me was a side-to-side motion that knocked down the fragile stuff. Then I'd use my pruner to snip each of the beefier stems. Evidently, I was one of the few that brought tools from home. Most folks didn't read the fine print on the web site and thought they couldn't bring stuff like that. It made my day a lot easier.

My enthusiasm had to get dialed back. I cleared too big a path. It was easy to fall into gardening mode where I knocked the weeds down to the dirt. Too much of that though and the land around the trail doesn't look wild enough. I cleared so much brush in one area that our trail leader thought people might use that ground instead of the real trail. A point of definition: the plants are not weeds. They are right where they are supposed to be. We humans simply needed to kill enough of them for so we could walk by. We strove for just enough order through a lot of chaos.

Twenty three volunteers spread out over a couple of miles with only four bosses meant that we could do whatever we wanted. Of course most folks that volunteer are conscientious types, so we tried to do good work. If I wasn't clearing brush, I was improving drainages or cleaning the trail of fallen branches and such.

The trail leaders walked through with candy and encouragement and eventually invited everyone to take a break and get together for lunch. One of the perks of working by the lake was that most folks came to us. Everyone was responsible for their own food, though there was always more chocolate available.

Sitting around at lunch I came to appreciate working in the trees. Evidently, some folks spent the morning in the unrelenting sunshine of the avalanche chute using loppers on the bushes. They were hot, beat, and looked to trade off with anyone. I don't know if anyone swapped with them. We'd uncovered enough jobs that no one was bored or finished. As we ate, we traded camping stories. Everyone agreed that rodents landing on your face at night are more frightening than bears that walk by unnoticed. It is unsettling though to see bear or cougar tracks outside your tent in the morning. We looked up at Baring and talked about how and if to get up it. Simply because it is there is not sufficient reason for some folks.

Eventually we drifted back to work. We agreed to take on some of the bigger tasks that would benefit from a group effort. A few of us went back to clean up the last of some other tasks first. There were a few more bushes that I wanted to kill.

Less than an hour later, I was done and headed back down the trail. There was a group tackling a job I never imagined. They were turning mud into dry dirt. Some low points on the trail become mud pits. The water doesn't drain correctly and lots of boots beat the dirt into slurry. To fix that someone gets the very messy task of digging out all of the mud until they reach hardpan or rock. Then the group takes on the heavy work of filling the hole with big rocks, like a French drain. After folks are muddy and sore it is time to find a good source of clean dirt, dig it out, haul it to the hole and pack it all in until it looks like every other bit of dry trail. All of that hard work gets camouflaged. How many times had I walked over so much hidden work? No wonder it all gets taken for granted; it is done so well that no one should be able to notice. Lots of good works get handled that way.

I was amazed when they described that process to me. I covered my reaction by making some facetious remark about them being almost done. A few minutes later, I was fifteen feet above the trail digging rocks out of the hillside. It takes a lot of rocks to fill a hole. Then it took a lot of dirt to cover the rocks. That's where I really got messy. We dug out rocks and passed them down to the trail.

Amidst all of that work we had to remember that one of the jobs was to call out "hiker!" whenever we spotted someone coming along the trail. Lots of people are savvy enough to watch out for themselves, but hikers also include the temporarily clueless like couples on dates, kids, pets, and people wrapped up in thoughts, the scenery or in-depth conversations. I get into that space often enough. Hitting them with a bone cracking rock would ruin everyone's day.

The time went fast. Good busy work will do that. Eventually everyone decided it was time to wander back to the trailhead. We did some odd jobs along the way. Sometimes we stopped to help another group finish up a task. Knowing what our group did made me more appreciative of the other groups' accomplishments. The best trail work blended so well that it had to be pointed out. I made dead plants and dug dirty holes. That was obvious. I was impressed with the folks that left their work site looking natural and wild, not like some recently vacated construction zone.

On the way out I had that general fatigue that isn't concentrated anywhere, but shows that everything has been used more than enough for one day. My brain mostly concentrated on not injuring my body with the tools I carried. I said that I appreciated the work done by others and that was true, but my mind was more focused on getting back to the car.

The trail bosses handed out free pop and cookies back at the trailhead. The sugar and caffeine were what I wanted for the drive home. There was a bit of chatter, but most folks drifted towards their cars and maybe a change of clothes.

The work was self-directed, so any aches or pains were self-inflicted. It was obvious that sore muscles would be around the next day or two, but we had helped out and that felt good.

Working on the trail and socializing with the rest of the group were almost enough to blank out the marvelous day. If the weather had been miserable, we would have noticed. We were lucky. The air was warm enough to get campers swimming. The sky was clear enough for nice views of the forest and the rock faces. The lake was the busiest I had seen it. Almost all of the campsites were filled and some folks were obviously there for a long stay. One group was in the midst of making a Frisbee golf course on the side of the hill. It was probably not a quiet night. I suspect there was a boom box somewhere in that crowd.

Nature wouldn't slow down for any of that. The rockfalls continued. The flowers worked hard. Trillium was already on the down side of its season. Bleeding hearts were in their prime. Ferns were way past fiddleheads and were big and leafy without losing that fresh bright green that they start the season with. I knew about the ferns because I whacked so many of them on my way to attacking thorny bushes like salmonberry and Devil's Club.

The valley was gorgeous. Enough snow remained high up to provide some relief and contrast with the deepening greens of the trees. The birds were very busy and probably very ticked at all of the racket we caused. Maybe they would be happy that we turned up lots of squirmy things where we dug up rocks. One snake was upset with us. As we walked out there was a three foot garter snake that looked impressive and confident. Instead of running away, it slithered off to the side and then rose up to watch us watch it. That was the only other wildlife besides the birds. I didn't even see any squirrels or chipmunks. Maybe they were too busy raiding the campers' food.

I'll probably sign up for another work crew. I'd like to get my own hardhat. It would be cheaper to buy one, but I'd rather earn it.

Summer was near and I wanted to spend some time camping and relaxing so I planned a second trip for June. My plan was to visit Barclay on my way to a night or two at Eagle. No one worked on that vertical bit of trail, but at least I had a better idea of how to get there. I especially wanted to get there in that other narrow window when camping is comfortable, but the crowds are stopped because the road to the back door is closed by snow.

June 16-18

Monday, June 16

June got July's weather. For a few days it was supposed to be gorgeously sunny and in the seventies. June is supposed to be cloudy and struggling through the sixties. Most of my household chores were done, so I skipped out for the rare opportunity of a couple of dry nights at the lake.

In May, Barclay was uninhabited. Lots of things let that happen and I didn't count on being that lucky again. It seemed unlikely that Barclay would be empty during fine weather after Memorial Day. I shifted my plan up a notch and decided to hike past Barclay and go up to Eagle Lake where there'd be fewer people. Besides, playing around in Paradise Valley and maybe climbing a ridge for a view sounded like fun. There was nothing but snow in the valley around Eagle last time, so I made sure I packed for hiking and camping on snow. Despite that, I hoped and guessed that at least one campsite was thawed out.

Helping a friend move five tons of rocks on Sunday meant I was in no hurry to get up on Monday. Instead of getting to the trailhead in the middle of the morning like usual, I got there just before noon. There were four cars in the parking lot when I got there. Four more cars showed up in the time it took me to change into hiking boots and load up my pack. Just like I thought, it was going to be busy at Barclay.

Maybe it was the season or maybe it was the time of day, but the lighting along the trail was more beautiful than before. The typically subdued first stretch that slides under the crowded canopy of trees had shafts of sunlight spotting small groups of ferns and tiny delicate flowers. The broad petals of the trillium were faded. Other plants took their turn and blossomed with little white petaled flowers no bigger than my thumbnail. Some were tiny spires of delicate white specks like little live sparklers. It was a very pleasant way to start the hike.

The trail looked different to me because of my work with the maintenance crew. I noticed it more than before and was happy with what we accomplished. Our work made me more aware of the heavy lifting that goes on by the folks who get paid. Compared to road construction, trail building is cheap, but my guess is that it is much harder. Heavy machinery doesn't fit on the trails. People have to use their muscles and sweat instead of hydraulics and diesels. Pry bars, shovels and maybe a chain saw have to get wielded by strong backs working in dirt, mud, streams, bushes, and around trees and boulders. I noticed how much dirt, rocks, and logs had to be moved to make a short, mostly flat, trail like the one to Barclay. The longer trails farther in were much more impressive accomplishments. The sections I worked on made me wish I had a tool or two along and the time for some touch up work.

It was such a pain to see that in the short time since our work was done, some group had wandered along the trail ripping up small trees by the roots, and shoved rotting stumps onto the trail. It was juvenile destruction; though for all I know the criminals were old and should know better. I grumped my way along cleaning up their mess. Families with small kids were hiking the trail and I didn't want them to run headlong into a branch and poke out an eye.

That's one reason I avoid popular trails. Most of the time the scenery that made them popular impresses me, but the irresponsible behavior of a few clueless individuals ruins that. Luckily, Mother Nature is very stout in such well watered and low altitude areas. In a couple of places, I was amazed to see that they tried torching living trees. They didn't succeed. Nature would continue but I was less forgiving.

Despite the busy parking lot, the lake wasn't very crowded. The families were very well behaved and some of them stopped where the kids got distracted. One family didn't make it past the footbridge. There was only one tent at the lake and one solo dayhiker. He decided it was time to go when he heard about the kids. Well-behaved children aren't necessarily quiet and he looked like the contemplative sort. We chuckled about the kids. We liked them and we were kids in our past, but they don't always aid quiet contemplation. He headed back down the trail and I kept moving along the lake.

The lake level was dropping very slowly. Each month through the winter, the lake level rose until the shoreline vanished and the tree roots were wet. The change was slight, but I noticed more beach and drier roots. The lake was losing water faster than the snowmelt was coming in. It looked so nice, and there was only one tent, so I considered ditching my plans for Eagle Lake in favor of Barclay. One tent more wouldn't be too much of a crowd. Curiosity won out. I wanted to see Eagle Lake and Paradise Meadow for more than just a dayhike.

Getting to Barclay was the easy part. The sharp turn to Eagle was a dramatic mental and physical shift. When I first hiked there, I noticed that in a mile and a half the trail gains fifteen hundred feet. It is actually steeper than that. The distance to Eagle Lake is a mile and a half. The high point on the trail is within the first mile, a little past Stone Lake. Fifteen hundred feet in a mile is a major grunt on well maintained trails. After the trail leaves Barclay it becomes a dotted line on the map. It isn't maintained or even well marked. Doing all of that with an overnight pack on didn't make it easier. The next hour or two were committed to grinding my way up the hill, occasionally getting lost, and finding my way again.

Along the way there were fine little vignettes of flowers, some orchids, and saplings with fresh growth, but I didn't stop to take a picture. I stored the images in my head, but not in the camera. I had no desire to strip off the backpack and rummage around in it on such a steep hill where I was never sure of my location. I was focused on route finding, not picture taking. Sometimes hiking is like that. There is a proverb about the journey being more important than the destination. In the afternoon on marginal trails, getting to camp is more important than enjoying the view. Communing with nature comes after you've made your way through it.

Down near Barclay the undergrowth was thick, but after a couple of hundred feet of elevation the gaps between the tree trunks opened up. Finding the route would have been much more difficult without the occasional long view under the trees. I spent a lot of time looking for any sign of footprints, trail tape, or cairns. Not seeing them didn't mean I was lost. There aren't many footprints early in the season and the weather can destroy trail marks. Stitching the trail together was a chore though.

I thought my trail work down below was poor because some bushes looked like they might grow back onto the trail. The trail to Eagle was much worse and made the trail to Barclay look like a manicured garden. After the path crossed a stream, I entered an area where the brush was so bad that I wanted long pants. The forest gave way to unshaded streambeds and avalanche chutes. There the bushes grew and fought each other for the sunshine. At least the trail was visible. I've been on some trails where the brush is so healthy that you find the trail by feeling along with your feet. It wasn't that bad, but it would get worse as the plants grew. In the meantime, there were enough thorns that my shins were scratched and bleeding. It wasn't life threatening, but it was a nuisance. Bugs were attracted to my mini-buffet of bloody scratches.

I groaned at the thought of the bugs waking up. Some folks don't like snakes. Some folks don't like rats. I don't like bugs. They get to me and yes, they bug me. I particularly hate it when they fly into my eyes and ears. It wasn't that bad yet and the trail wasn't too bushy yet, so I counted my blessings. July would have a worse combination of bushes and bugs.

I'd climb a bit and stop. Then I'd climb a bit and stop. Then I'd look around for the next trail clue and guess where to climb next. To the purists out there, I know it wasn't true climbing because no rope or exposure was involved. There were very few times when handholds were necessary. But there is a group of trails that are steeper than they should be. Whether you want to call them hikes or climbs is up to you. My lungs and heart didn't make fine distinctions. They were working hard and didn't care what I called my efforts. They wanted to see the flat land in the meadows and then fall down in camp.

Past the rockfalls, the trail heads up into a gap in the ridge. Below the gap, a stream flows through under a pile of rocks and fallen trees. It was a dicey area when it was covered with snow. All that snow was gone and what remained was much easier to navigate. That was a good enough excuse to celebrate with a break. It looked like I was in a rock garden.

A couple of women came down the trail. They were so wrapped up in their conversation that I startled them by simply standing there. It is always good to get a report on the trail ahead. According to them, Eagle Lake was snow-free and was very close. I thought it was at least another half mile. Most hikers are terrible at guessing distances and for some folks a half mile is close. People heading down think the way up is short and people heading up think they've gone a long way. But I thought they were confused about Eagle Lake. That is when the expert cruised through. He was a solo hiker who barely slowed down as he told us that they had mistaken Stone Lake for Eagle Lake. I thought Stone Lake was behind me and thought that maybe they had wandered off to some other seasonal pond. He said I didn't know what I was talking about. He didn't stay to chat. Maybe he didn't like the way, or the fact, that I disagreed with him. They were disappointed because they realized that they probably missed Eagle Lake.

Two minutes later, I realized he was right. I hadn't made it to Stone Lake yet. That was a letdown for me because I realized how much farther I had to go. It's not like every place is marked when you get there. I blamed my mistake on exhaustion. It was all the fault of the five tons of rock we'd moved the previous day. That was my excuse, but it wasn't the reason. I hadn't thought through where I really was on the trail. Hiking while that tired is not a good idea. After the trailhead, clear thinking is a necessity. Muddy thinking is dangerous.

A few steps farther, but really a few hundred feet, I was at Stone Lake. The lake was totally snow-free, but the ground around it was squishy. It didn't look like a good campsite for a human, but it looked like a great place for frogs, bugs and salamanders. I left them to their luxuriously soggy neighborhood.

Paradise Meadow came into view as I passed through the minor gap in the little ridge behind Stone Lake. The valley was almost completely green. The snow was gone so what wasn't green was the brown of bark or the grey of rock. With the exception of the wildflowers, the meadow in springtime looked surprisingly like it did in the fall. But springtime was the time for color. None of the blossoms were big enough to stand out on their own. Instead, millions of little flowers highlighted the view with soft pinks and whites.

I stood there looking at a series of gardens. Each was defined by a small cluster of stout trees huddled on every bit of raised earth. At the base of the trees was a skirt of heather beginning to hint at blossoms. Spread out across the rest of the meadow was a carpet of grasses and flowers far brighter than the islands of trees and heathers. Winding through in random paths were clear streams in narrow channels with steep banks crowned with overhanging grasses. It looked wonderful. I simply had to find my way through it to dry land.

From the low ridge above Stone Lake to Eagle Lake, the trail was mostly flat and definitely muddy. My snowshoes were only going to be useful if I used them to keep from sinking into the mud. I should have listened to myself and tried that. After two or three failed attempts at picking my way around some very soggy soil, my boots were plastered with mud. The waterproofing didn't matter when the water came in over the top and down around my socks. I gave in to the mess and stopped worrying about avoiding the mud. My boots weren't going to get clean and dry until they had a chance to sit in the sun. I mucked my way to the lake and apologized for the erosion. At least I didn't contribute to the detours through the heather. Which is the best route to follow in a place like that?

I wanted to take some pictures as I sploshed my way along, but dropping my pack into the mud to get out the camera was not going to happen. It was easier to stand there and mentally absorb the colors of the blossoms. I could come back with camera in hand after I made camp. Where were the bugs? I expected to be inundated, but only a few of them went by.

When I crossed the last stream at the edge of the meadow, I was glad to be out of the mud. It seems strange that the land closest to the lake is drier than the meadow farther out, but some trick of geology surrounds that end of Eagle Lake with a dry forest floor that slowly rises to the lakeshore. There isn't much undergrowth and there were dry campsites. I was very relieved and grateful.

In May, Eagle Lake had entire shattered trees and fallen rocks lying on the lake's snow-capped surface. I looked out on a lake that was totally thawed. Those rocks were on the lake bottom and the logs were either floating towards the outlet or waterlogged and stuck in the mud. Spring was busy pumping out enough pollen to paste the lakeshore with a yellow film that was thick enough to calm the waves. Back from the shoreline the ground was either quickly melting snow in a chilly puddle, or dirt that was open and dry.

I was alone and had my pick of campsites. That was more luxury again. I dropped my pack and went shopping for real estate. The best campsite was beside the outlet and had a view of the lake and Merchant Peak. It was mid afternoon and I made camp. It felt good to stop and relax in peaceful solitude.

Knowing that the mountain across the water was Merchant was a new piece of knowledge. I finally learned the name of the peak. I rarely know much about an area when I hike into it for the first time. Learning the names was the first step. As soon as I learn one thing, I get more questions. Is Merchant a geologic and maybe volcanic cousin to Baring? Undoubtedly, someone with more affinity for research and a much better memory would know the names of all the local peaks and understand the local zoology, botany, and geology. I learn incrementally. The blanks in my internal maps had been drawn in over the months of visits. In June, they got labels. Knowing a name doesn't make the thing prettier, but it does make it more memorable.

Setting up camp was easy except for one task. Ideally, campers are supposed to hang their food from a tree branch that is high enough up and far enough out that a bear can't reach it. We don't want the bears to start thinking that people equal food, eh? The books I've read show nice little pictures of a line thrown up and over a branch. The branch should be something like twelve feet up and six feet out. You clip the food bag to the line and haul up the bag out of reach. That sounds so simple. The trees in those books must not grow in the Cascades. Many species shed their lower branches leaving more than twenty feet of bare trunk. If there are any branches down low they are usually either too low or too ready to snap off. It took me thirty minutes to get a line over the nearest good branch. It was near the limit of how high I could throw the line, so most of my tosses fell short, bounced off the tree trunk, or wrapped around some twig on the branch and got stuck. About a dozen times I had to yank the line out of the tree, which sent the weighted end screaming back at me. I know experts can do it in one throw, but none of them were along for the hike.

I was tired. Moving rocks one day and climbing with a pack the next wore me out. I settled into the tent to read and nap away from the afternoon mosquito patrols. They weren't swarming, but there were enough of them to make relaxed reading difficult. It was much easier reading in the tent where I didn't have to spend most of my time digging them out of my ears or swatting them from my neck.

Eagle Lake is set into more of a bowl than Barclay is. On the left, a ridge climbs up behind the cabin to become Merchant Peak. From there a spur ridge forms the far wall across the lake and that wall gradually climbs and turns around the lake to become Townsend Mountain. The ridge extends and climbs for another mile or so before the peak of Townsend caps the ridge over Paradise

Meadow. That continuous bit of geology makes a nice backdrop for the lake. It also blocks some of the wind. Besides the mosquitoes, the only other noise was the water flowing through the outlet. It was a fine evening. My fatigue made it easier to relax and quietly soak up the environment. After dinner, I left the rainfly off the tent and watched the sky darken past the trees.

It was near the Solstice. In one week it would happen and a few Druids would celebrate. For me it meant light late into the evening and an early dawn. I didn't expect to see the sun until late morning though. The ridges and thick forest would block a lot of light. There won't be much sunshine driving me out of my sleeping bag.

I realized that an early start might be useful. I planned to scramble up Townsend Mountain. Originally I considered skiing it, but the avalanches and rock faces cured me of that notion. There didn't seem to be a clear hiking path or route up it, so I wanted to take more time than usual getting through the bushes and trees at its base. With sixteen hours of daylight, I could sleep past dawn, have lots of time for breakfast, and still have an early start. The lazy part of me thought that maybe I'd simply stay in camp to read and write. That was doubtful.

Tuesday, June 17

Sleeping in sounded like a good idea, but the birds had a different idea. It was hard to sleep at the heart of hummingbird central. Every few minutes, the sound of a huge mutant bumblebee buzzed the head of my tent. Something there looked like food to them and they'd thrum up, hover about, and then fling off into the forest. It was a unique alarm clock that I turned off by getting up.

The pollen piled along the shoreline the previous day flowed back out across the lake during the night. Instead of a thick paste on the shoreline, the entire surface of the lake was slightly yellow. I was amazed my hay fever hadn't gone bonkers.

The pollen drifted around because the wind died near dawn. As the wind died so did the mosquito barrier. They weren't a menace, but they were bad enough that I put on long pants and a jacket as armor against their bites. Breakfast was the familiar camp routine of stick a spoonful of oatmeal into my mouth and then swat at the bugs. Repeat until the dishes are clean or the diner is insane.

Before I left camp, I studied the map a bit. I was surprised to notice that the peak of Townsend was only slightly shorter than the spire of Baring and the peak of Merchant. It is a mountain, but it looked much more accessible because its character is that of a long open ridge with a few high spots.

Most of the hillside was snow-free. A few snowfields were scattered about where the slope was shallower. On anything steeper, the snow had tried to stick, failed, and at some point slid. Piles of avalanche debris extended to the lake below the rock outcrops. The avalanches were done for the season. Any snow movement was going to be little trickles of water from melted snow. The rest of the hillside was a blotchy mix of rocks, shrubs, and small trees.

I didn't know of a trail to the top and couldn't see an obvious route, so I stood in camp for a long time visually stitching together an approach. My best plan used the remnants of an avalanche or two and some not too steep rock faces. I also kept in mind that nothing required me to get there and that I could turn around if things got too uncomfortable. Fun was more important than peak bagging.

A trail around the lake would have been handy. Any fisherman's path was hidden and useless until the remaining snow melted, the lake drained a bit, and the occasional mud puddle dried up. I started bushwhacking within a hundred yards of camp. The bushes were thick, green and growing fast. Their leaves were fresh and not fully grown. The branches were supple which meant they whipped back at me as I pushed through them. The ground was wet. I walked on melting snow, through slushy water, and on the muddy edges of large puddles. Branches buried by a season of snow wanted to spring up as the snow softened. So branches were sometimes popping me from below or a foot would punch through snow into a tangle of shrubbery.

I pulled my way through bushes, around trees, and waded through buzzing berry bushes. The bees were busy and I hoped I didn't disturb them. I called them thumblebees because they were the size of my thumb. They probably wouldn't sting me unless I gave accidentally grabbed one, but I am a klutz so that was a possibility.

From lake to peak was a two thousand foot change in altitude. I was glad for an early start. That much bushwhacking and that much climbing could take a lot of time.

Getting to the base of the ridge was enough work that I wondered if I hadn't taken on too tough a task. The best places to stand were on piles of avalanched snow. Their view wasn't blocked by trees and avalanched snow can be incredibly firm. I stood on one and looked up the hill to review and revise my route. The snow was the best path available, but the top of each slide ended in either a stream or a pile of bushes. On each slope, I had to guess ahead of time where to exit the slide to make my way over to its neighbor. My battle with the bushes at the base also changed my estimate of how tall the shrubbery was. Getting from one slide to the next involved weaving my way through slide alder and salmonberry that was over my head. Navigation was not easy and I relied on the simple adages: "Keep climbing" and "No Stupid Mistakes".

Hiking through the slide alder where I had branches in my face and under my feet made me appreciate the openness and traction of rocks and snow. I aimed for the stretches of tilted rock faces. There the route finding was easier and my feet would actually contact ground, not be suspended and balanced on a never-ending raft of slick sticks, roots and leaves.

Slabs of granite bedrock make for easy travel. I only had to fight gravity and look for hand and foot holds. But while rock is hard, it isn't always solid. The fractured and tumbled rocks scattered across the slabs were a pain. Maneuvering through them was an unrelenting mental exercise of continually testing which route to pick and which stone to trust. A hiker walking on them can kick some rockslides free again. Occasionally the underlying surface was wet from snowmelt. Sometimes it was like having a staircase to walk up. I got by with very little need for handholds. But in the wet and gravelly places, each step took much more time. Pebbles on wet slabs of rocks are only slightly more stable than ball bearings on oiled sheets of steel. Each foot placement was tested before I set my weight on it. Mountain goats make it look so easy.

I was glad to be on the rocks. The views were nicer and the air was fresher. It was much easier to take a break while standing on solid footing. It wasn't long before I was above the tallest trees. They stayed in the valley and around the lake. A few hundred feet up the hill and I was above them. As I got higher, my breaks happened where I could see down the valley and across the lake to the neighboring ridges. The valley, lake and basin were nicely laid out for my viewing and the wind came by to blow away the insects. The fresh meadow, the pollen dusted lake, and the rocks wet with snowmelt were all mine, or at least no one else was there. I was alone in the valley.

The expanse of rocks stopped a few hundred feet below the ridgeline. My altimeter was dead, so my best way to guess my progress was by looking across the valley and lake to Baring, Merchant and the surrounding ridges. The peak of Townsend was almost as high as its neighbors, so I watched to see where I was relative to them. The views past the local ridges began to open up with snowy folds in the earth stacking themselves towards the horizon. Below each snow capped ridge was a green valley that suggested two seasons in close proximity.

My fear of heights kicked in when I looked down at Eagle Lake. I was impressed with my efforts, but I also noticed that the lake was a long way down there. The slope was steep enough to let me bounce most of the way if I tripped.

It was like looking down some of those black diamond ski slopes where you can't see past the lip. I couldn't see the entire slope below me. The rock face below me blocked part of the view like a cliff. I knew it wasn't that abrupt because I had climbed it without any gear besides handholds and footsteps, but going back down it didn't look appealing. Skiing that slope was beyond my ability, but I know folks who would love the chance. So much for my ski dreams.

There were more berry bushes above the rocks. The change in altitude was enough to shrink the shrubs. Instead of the head high shrubbery below, I waded through knee-high bushes. There were acres of blueberry bushes. The bears would have a happy harvest in a few months. The land buzzed. Picking my way through those hidden footholds without stepping on a bee kept me occupied enough that I didn't notice the ridge crest until I was fifty feet below it. Even then I didn't believe it was there. I've been tricked by false summits and don't celebrate until I am on top and can see down into the next valley.

Awesome views happen. In the full meaning of the word, every direction I looked was a view that gave me a feeling of awe. The view to the horizon was a relentless series of ridges punctured by peaks. It drew my eye up, out and around 360 degrees. The day was clear and my view was long. I was overwhelmed with all the places laid out before me. I should know many of them, but hadn't seen them from that point of view and there were so many of them that I was overwhelmed. I concentrated on identifying one, and the one beside it would distract me, and the one beside that would continue the trend until I was looking over my shoulder.

Below me, on the Eagle Lake side of the ridge, spring was busily running into summer. Past the sharp drop into the next valley was a change into late winter. Snow covered almost everything. Along the ridge were the remnants of cornices that were ten feet thick of hard packed snow. Melt water slowly trickled off their tips. Below, the snowfields were warped, creased and veined with the patterns of internal melting. Two lakes were down there and they were at the stage where the shoreline was melted, but the snowcaps remained. The snowcaps were melting too. The veins of melt water carved deep enough into the snow to show lake water in the midst of the cap. I remembered that Eagle Lake went from a snowcap stout enough to hold up trees and boulders to completely thawed in less than a month. Seeing a lake's snowcap just as it broke through is a very temporary and special sight.

I pulled out the camera for the first time on the climb. I fell into shooting a full circle panorama because after each shot I wanted the one next to it too. I wanted to take it all in. There was no view of humanity. I was alone and the world was beautiful. After a while, I put the camera away and stood there trying to absorb the view and the experience. I knew I wouldn't be able to remember what all of my senses noticed, but I tried anyway.

The summit was a long ridge walk away. Small gaps in ridges can be easily overlooked until they reveal themselves as moats and impenetrable defenses of the summit. There was however, a hint of a trail along the top of the ridge. I started hiking along it towards the summit while hoping it led me around any barriers. There were no guarantees, but I didn't worry. The summit would be neat, but the views from the ridge were more than good enough for me.

All the way up I kept in mind getting all the way down. For safety and fun, I called my wife to tell her where I was. I am fascinated with the ability to make phone calls from places that are so remote. I thought someone should know where I was in case something happened. Besides, it's also fun to share places like that. While I talked to her, my description made me look more intently at the view. Earlier I had looked straight at Rainer and hadn't noticed it. Describing the scene to Kaye made me look through the haze and spot the mountains on the far horizon. To the north were Baker and Glacier, and to the east I convinced myself I could see Stuart. After our talk, I took another break and got out the map. The majority of the peaks were far beyond my map's borders.

Some people have a rough time understanding why hikers and climbers are so willing to spend so much effort at getting so far from the comforts of home. Words and photos can only hint at the experience of standing in a place like that while the mind scurries to memorize the moment. I'd like to think that I can convey the feeling, but know that experience is always far richer than any description.

As I hiked along, I found more wildlife than I had seen on the climb. Two ptarmigans in spring feathers chased each other around on the snow. I couldn't decide if it was courtship or defense of territory. They were fun to watch in either case. Their coats were mottled as they changed with the seasons. They bopped around on foot along the boundary between the berry bushes and the cornices of snow and looked like some slapstick routine.

The rest of the life up there was much smaller, and much more numerous. Flocks of little birds wheeled around and errant bees and flies buzzed by. If they got too high, they got blown into the next valley. I didn't understand what they found up there that wasn't easier to get just a hundred feet below the ridge, but then I don't have a bird's brain. Life on the ridge was hectic.

The ridge got serious as it approached the summit. The scant hiker's trail vanished in a steep boulder field that looked like broken bits of an old fortress. The rocks were large and black, and not always pleased with their position. Car sized rocks moved when I stepped on them. My way uphill became precarious. Geologically young ridges falling down are not an academic abstraction when they are moving under your feet.

That's when my cell phone rang. Keep in mind that my cell phone rarely rings. Most of the time I am not sure why I have it turned on. I thought my wife might be calling me back, so I stabilized myself and fished out the phone. It was a business call. I get business calls about once a month. I want my business to do well enough, but talking about advertising rates in a mobile boulder field at nearly 6,000 feet didn't seem like the best use of my time. The saleswoman was very understanding and agreed to call back in a few days when I was some place less adventurous. Being able to use a phone anywhere is not always a good thing.

I made it past the boulders and found a small peak along the ridge. Rather than act as a haven, standing there was only slightly more comforting than climbing the boulders. The peak was a loose pile of rocks that jutted out from the ridge and ended in sheer drops into the next valley. It looked like a strong kick would topple the pile. A small stout bush was rooted at the pinnacle. It was actually a stunted tree: a natural bonsai. That meant there was some dirt there, which made the ground look a little more stable, but I didn't use it as proof of safety. I weighed more than a foot high bonsai. Despite a lack of stability, it did have one of the nicest settings for a bonsai. The tree was bordered by rocks that were about the same size as the tree. They were black, rough, and sporadically covered with lichens. Beyond the tree was a view north across the heart of the Cascades. Looking south I saw the north sides of ridges and they were covered with snow. Looking north past the tree I saw the ridges' south sides which were covered with green. Every direction was framed with a clear blue sky that extended to the horizon.

I took a photograph of Eagle Lake's valley to show how far I climbed and also a photo of the rest of the ridge to record why I didn't go farther. The true peak was that much farther, higher and exposed. The ridge below the peak was stark, stacked, vertical black rock. It looked ominous and too exposed for me. Others might know of a good solid route, but I knew I'd gone far enough. It was time to turn back.

Eyeing the routes back to the lake, I saw some alternatives to my uphill route. I had traversed far along the ridge, but the best looking path was directly below me instead of back the way I came. It dropped down a nearly constant slope through an open field straight into the valley, but added a long slog through the meadow. That was better than fighting the bushes and slippery rocks of my uphill route. A long scree field with occasional shrubbery started about five hundred feet below the berry bushes. Scree fields are open fields of rocks that are broken pieces of the mountain. Sometimes the rocks are the size of cars. Sometimes the rocks shrink to become gravel. What lay below me was a long field of foot-sized rocks. The rocks are rarely stable. Every footstep had to be watched and tested, but very little grows there, so it is easy to navigate. At the bottom I'd have to bushwhack, but it's safer to bushwhack on the flat than down a steep hill through slide alder.

Climbing down was a simple, but tiring and tiresome task. The monotony of watching each step was hard to fight. Rarely was there a time when the rocks felt stable enough for me to stop and enjoy the view. That was a pity. The weather was excellent. A few clouds built up, probably from rapidly evaporating snow-melt, but they dissipated quickly. The temperature was warm enough for lots of sweat, but the wind came up to blow off the bugs and keep me cool.

I dropped two thousand feet in an hour. Evidently I was quick at testing each step.

Near the valley floor, the scree field flattened and ended in a mix of tree branches. I knew Eagle Lake was off to my right, so I angled that way. There was a gap in the trees, but there was no sign of a trail. The route I chose plunged me into thick tangles of branches and pockets of undergrowth within the first hundred feet. It was messy and scratchy. The forest wasn't much different than the forest near the campsite but the undergrowth was much heavier. Maybe campers tromping around made that big difference.

It was a novel way to see parts of the valley that normally I'd avoid. Evidently, my dead reckoning was a bit off because instead of finding the lake I wandered too far left and down into the muddy valley. That was a messy, but pleasant, accident. I popped out of some thick mess of bushes and found small meadows of avalanche lilies and wide patches of some unrecognizable four petaled white flower. They evidently loved soggy feet because their toes were in mud. There was plenty of daylight left so getting back to camp in the shortest time possible wasn't necessary. I was in the valley and safe so I took some time to wander through the muddy gardens and enjoy the flowers. It was a peaceful walk and it was fun visiting each new garden. A few mud puddles and scratchy bushes later I stumbled onto dry land and was quickly back in camp.

I am glad there wasn't an established route up Townsend. It is refreshing to find places that get visited so rarely that a trail isn't paved into the dirt by thousands of boot prints. Land that gets visited can still be wild, but a very established trail feels awfully civilized after a bout of bushwhacking. Some trails are so refined that they act as reminders of a link back to asphalt and strip malls. Surprisingly little untraveled land exists, so I content myself with finding places that have the slightest of trails and the widest views of unblemished lands. At times like those I wonder what the first humans thought when they stood there. Were they impressed with the view and the plenty or dismayed with the obstacles before them?

It was barely past noon and I was tired enough to willingly collapse for the rest of the day. My early start and surprisingly quick return meant I had a long lazy afternoon ahead of me. The only thing left to do was nap, read, write, and take on a few camp chores. I drank a lot of water.

When I looked for campsites, I thought about camping up on the ridge. Despite the enormous amount of snow available for melting and drinking, I am glad I didn't try camping there. Very little up there is flat. Some folks will bivouac there, and the view is worth it, but I was much more comfortable down by the lake. I had elbowroom and didn't have to worry about rolling over into the next valley in the middle of the night.

After a relaxing afternoon, it got dark. The sun slid below the ridge and none of the peaks caught sunshine anymore. There were a few more sounds in the woods, but I couldn't tell if they were campers, bears, or falling tree branches. I napped so much that day that I thought I wouldn't sleep well that night. Oh well, I could read as long as my batteries lasted.

It was a good day.

Wednesday, June 18

Glorious June weather doesn't last. At dusk, two small high clouds had caught some of the last sun. Around midnight I watched the moonrise through the trees so the sky must have been clear. Sometime between then and dawn, the clouds came back. When I pulled myself out of my sleeping bag in the morning, the air felt damp and the sky was overcast. On an earlier visit, a member of the Forest Service told me that the area was within ten or fifteen inches of rainfall of being a temperate rain forest. The clouds proved his point. The last weather forecast I heard suggested rain late on Wednesday. The clouds suggested they might get an early start.

I wasn't worried. Glimpses through the lower cloud deck showed another higher, brighter cloud deck that didn't seem threatening. Maybe what I saw was morning fog under a partly cloudy sky. Five minutes later, before I started making breakfast, I turned towards the lake and watched a cloud spill over the ridge and dive towards the lake. Half of Merchant Peak was hidden. That was temporary. A few minutes later, it was back in full view again. Ten minutes later, the only land I could see was the shoreline. Anything higher was lost to fog. The forest shrunk as clouds rolled up the valley and cut the view short. Mountain weather changes fast.

I didn't rush, but I did limit my actions to finishing breakfast, packing, and leaving. I didn't want to hike down in the rain. Less than an hour later, I was gone. I'd hoped to look back up at Townsend to pick out my routes, but that was a lost cause. The fog shrunk Paradise Meadow into a series of small gardens. Their backdrop was a featureless grey instead of a rugged hillside. With the clouds in the way, it was hard to imagine the mountainous ridges surrounding the heathers and spring flowers. Instead of looking at spreads of meadows backed by mountain walls, my eyes saw a series of gardens and groves that looked more cozy than grand. Back through the mud puddles and squishy ground I went. It made for a mostly quiet morning exit.

By accident and sometimes by design, I never took the exact same route up and down that trail. On the way down, I found another set of trail markers that crossed unfamiliar territory. That kept the hike from getting boring I guess.

The first few hundred feet were the worst. Getting through the wet spots and past the rocks was easier than the climb down Townsend, but it required the same attention to every footstep. I was relieved when I crossed back into the forest. The dotted line trail looked better than anything I had walked on for the previous day or so. That's also where I got below the cloud deck. The top half of Baring and all of the surrounding ridges were covered in cloud, but I could finally get valley glimpses again. After taking in the limited view, I concentrated on getting down to Barclay.

That was a lot of hill to get down. As I lost elevation the view through the trees changed from clouds, to distant trees, to treetops near eye level. That was the best way for me to check my progress. Eventually the view was of the lake and I was back in a comfort zone. I was on a solid line trail with the hill behind me.

No one was at the lake. Even in June, visiting the lake during the middle of the week meant solitude. I expected crowds or at least a few visitors after Memorial Day. I didn't complain. Quietly I made my way along the lake until I reached a campsite by the shore. I took a break, finally got out of my bug and brush armor jacket, and enjoyed looking at the quiet water. The clouds were temperamental. They drifted around without blowing off or settling in.

The walk out was more of a treat than I hoped for. The lighting was bright and diffuse. It sounds corny, but the flowers really did seem brighter. They were a pleasure to look at. I made it a slow and easy walk so I could appreciate the view and take some pictures. By walking slowly, I walked quietly and saw more things than usual. The creatures were more noticeable because I was quiet and not distracted by grand views. They didn't do anything unexpected, but it can be fun watching little creatures with amazingly tiny brains scurrying around for a living.

The trailhead was empty. My car was alone. The weather forecast probably scared everyone away. I had not seen another human for 48 hours. Maybe the area wasn't as busy as its reputation suggested.

For July, I thought I might try to find the crowds by spending a summer weekend at Barclay. I expected lots of people and noise. Which was worse, that no one knows about a place and it is safe but unappreciated, or everyone knows about it but some folks that visit it also trash it?

July

Monday, July 7

Plans for a thirteen mile walk through Seattle's neighborhoods fell through despite a forecast for excellent weather. I couldn't waste such good weather sitting inside. If I stayed home to do chores, I would be distracted the whole time thinking about the fine weather up high. Without a lot of preparation, I decided to go on a hike. Spontaneous situations like that are great examples of why I like picking one destination for a while. On very short notice, I knew where I would go and what I would need.

I filled the hole in my schedule with an idea that lived in the back of my head. The back door fisherman's trail into Eagle Lake intrigued me whenever I heard about it. I wanted to try it, but because it was dismissed in one of the guidebooks, I originally looked down on it. Of course, for years I also ignored the hike to Barclay because it was too short and shallow. That bit of prejudice was proved wrong, so maybe my opinion of the backdoor route was equally misguided. It looked like I'd finally found a good opportunity to satisfy my curiosity. The trail was supposed to be easy, flat and short so I planned on a quick hike.

The access to the route is from the road that winds up the next valley past Baring: Beckler River road. The unofficial trailhead was only four straight miles from the official one at Barclay, but there were tens of miles of roads between the two. The terrain forced great contortions into the road.

The timing was right. Bushes shouldn't be very large above a few thousand feet in July. Unmaintained trails are best traveled before the bushes grow and eat the trail. By the end of the summer, it could be a maze of branches. In general, if a trail isn't on the Forest Service's agenda, maintenance is unreliable. If boots can't trample the growth fast enough, the trail vanishes. Of course, sometimes that is a good thing.

The Washington Trails Association web site usually only has trail reports for the official trails.

There was no real reason to expect to see a report from Eagle Lake. I got lucky. Not only was there a trip report about the back door trail to Eagle, but the author gave a detailed description of how to find the trailhead. He missed it the first time and wanted to save others from the same mistakes. For his second attempt, he spent the time to research and record the right way to get there. He even included landmarks that propped up if you took the wrong turn. I printed out his directions. Hopefully they would save me his frustrations.

It was the Monday after the Fourth of July. The weekdays after a major holiday are usually quiet in the hills. Lots of folks camp during the holiday and run back home to work before Monday shows up. The folks that find quiet usually wait out the human storm for a day or two more. I was unlucky. I managed to get behind the one car headed up the hill. Most of the Forest Service roads are really logging roads. You didn't think they were built for hikers did you? Logging roads are rough, narrow and hug every curve in the hillside. The truck in front of me was an old pickup, so I guessed he was a logger going to check a future clearcut.

Danged if that truck didn't stay in front of me and take the same turns I had to take. There were enough spur roads that I was sure he would peel off onto one of them. Nope. It hadn't rained recently, so I ate dust every time I got within a hundred yards of him. He was not in a hurry. At one point, he stopped so his passenger could get out and help him steer the truck around a fallen tree. Luckily, my SUV was skinny enough to squeeze by the tree without guidance, just a bit of hope.

A few miles later, my view of his bumper hadn't changed. We snuck around a major boulder that narrowed the road and forced us to drive close to the edge of a cliff. I wondered if the road was too adventurous and risky for my curiosity. The optimist in me always hoped that there were no more obstacles, so it convinced me to continue. The pessimist worried about falling hundreds of feet into a river.

Hiking was going to be easy after that drive.

Some intersections on Forest Service roads might have signs. I came across a point where the gravelly road split into two more gravel paths. A lot of hope and map reading was involved. One road led up into a hairpin and one dropped toward a ravine. The description on the web site mentioned something like that. It sounds odd, but the only true test was to follow the wrong road until it obviously went the wrong way. It had the clearer landmark. Driving to trailheads is not always a straightforward task, and finding a trail that wasn't official was understandably tougher.

I turned down the road and had to pull over within a few hundred yards. The pickup was coming back up the road. Luckily, I was able to find a wider patch of gravel so there was enough room for both of us. As he got closer, we rolled down our windows. We were both curious about why the other driver was there. I was hunting for the landmark bridge. He wanted to know if I was hunting for the trailhead. We laughed when we realized that we were using each other's reports from the Washington Trails web site. The Internet makes it a small world.

He had driven down to the bridge to double check his posted description so we knew we were in the right place. We drove back to the intersection to park the vehicles and hike as a trio.

The Internet has strange influences. Because of our postings, we already knew something about each other. Being weekday hikers meant we had even more in common. We started that hike more as friends than strangers. Of course, friends know more about each other than we did so there was plenty to talk about as we swapped hiking stories and trail reports. That was almost enough to distract us from the bushes that snagged our pants or hit us in the face.

The trail was not in good repair. It was actually in good shape for a trail that didn't officially exist. In comparison to a Forest Service trail though, the trail to Eagle Lake was lacking. It also wasn't totally abandoned. Someone with a chain saw had been through within the last few months. We speculated that it was either the cabin's owners or the Forest Service's fire crews. Neither had to worry about making the trail pretty or straight, only passable. Gaps between bushes and beaten earth led up and around tree roots, trunks, over boulders and rarely held a straight line.

Some botanist can tell me why hiking through brush seemed to be hotter work than hiking along the road. All that I knew was that it was miserable work. It was hot and muggy hiking through the treeless patches of shrubs. I think it was an old clearcut. My sweat absorbed the dirt and mixed with my sunblock. Branches scratched and whipped about as we pushed our way through. The footing was hidden with growth and uneven enough to make us slip. Looking up for a view was useless. The branches were in front of our eyes and there were very few comfortable places to stand. Throw in some bugs and you get the picture.

Ads selling hiking gear rarely show the conditions we were in. In the catalogs and advertisements, hikers are clean and dry walking along a ridge surrounded by awesome views and wildflowers. Their heads are turned up to catch the sun and the wind is blowing through their hair. That is a good description of my ridge walk along Townsend, though with a lot more sweat, no cosmetics and definitely no hair blowing around. Through the back door into Eagle, we kept our heads down to keep the branches out of our eyes while we looked through the brush for the next place to step. Every few seconds the branches won when I was distracted by a cobweb in my face or a bug that needed swatting. Don't think it was a terrible ordeal, but it wasn't like we strolled along whistling while feeling peacefully in tune with nature.

Getting under the trees was a treat. Within a few feet, the canopy was thick enough to keep the air cool and the undergrowth under control. We had elbow-room and the shade felt good. There weren't any grand vistas, but I was happy enough looking at a forest of massive trees. If I was a better bird watcher, or at least a better bird listener, I probably could have noticed a change in the feathered population. I knew there were birds back in the bushes, but it was easier to notice the birds in the forest. We didn't see much in either place, but we listened to their song more after we got under the trees. Fewer distractions meant more time to enjoy what was there.

It is a slightly embarrassing admission that after twenty years of hiking I can't identify many of the trees or birds. It doesn't bother me much. I don't need to know something's name to like the way it looks or sounds. I might not get a job as a naturalist, but that is not my goal, so I am not worried.

Under the trees, the hiking was easier. The trail was easier to follow, but contorted and fragmented enough to obviously be unofficial.

Columnar trunks spread out around us leaving long views of thick sticks. Occasionally a slice was cut through the forest. Maybe a massive tree fell and nothing replaced it. Pocket views of Townsend Mountain popped out and revealed much clearer terrain and sunshine.

My view of Townsend was definitely colored by my climb of it. Climbing a peak does that to me. After climbing Mt. Rainier, it was no longer a cardboard cutout pasted on the horizon. It was much more three-dimensional, immensely larger, and alive. Looking at Townsend was similar though on a much smaller scale. It became much more captivating. Each view was a review of where I had been, or places I missed. I tried to envision what other parts of it looked like. I saw routes to avoid and routes to try.

That is one of the things that fascinates me about climbing mountains. Getting to the top of some peak or ridge causes lasting changes in the way I view the world. Sometimes the change is something as trivial as learning what the view is like from there. Sometimes though, it makes me realize the scale of the planet and my place on it. Small mountains are immensely larger than any building and they frequently provide views of larger mountains. I feel humbly tiny. That feeling came back simply from looking back up at a ridge climbed weeks before. Is that how the astronauts feel after they've seen the world from space? Is that the feeling non-hikers are missing out on? Does that explain why some folks don't recognize that nature isn't remote from them? Nature is not the stuff outside the asphalt. We poured asphalt onto Nature. Nature is there and everywhere, even if we can't see it. Civilization is merely the thin and temporary veneer that we've applied to the world.

A shake of my head and those kinds of thoughts were knocked back to my subconscious. I brought myself back to the familiar routine of a hike: the pleasant pastime of conversation and the mechanics of eating, hydrating and making sure we weren't lost.

The fisherman's trail was described as flat and short. That is a relative description. Compared to the route up from Barclay it is short and flat, but it gained about five hundred feet of elevation in about two miles. That isn't steep, but it isn't flat either. Think in terms of walking the stairs up a five hundred foot tall building and it sounds like a lot. The hike to Eagle Lake is very similar to the hike into Barclay. Because it wasn't a constant grade, it also meant that portions were steep enough to make us sweat and encourage us to appreciate breaks when we took them. Consider the source as well. Three old guys might think the trail had steep sections. Three young guys might think the entire trail was flat.

The good news was that when we got to Paradise Meadow we joined up with the official Eagle Lake trail where views and flowers were easier to appreciate. That made it worth our efforts. The bad news was that as we got closer to Paradise Meadows there were mud and bugs. Aside from major bushwhacking detours along the ridge, the best way to Eagle Lake was through the meadow where lots of water meant muck and biting insects.

Rather than fight the mud in the meadow and ruin my boots, I decided to try a different tactic. I switched to sandals. They were light, open, and easy to wash. Some will lament that I trampled habitat, but any hiker making progress is doing that. In areas as muddy as that meadow, the other choice is to try one of the many detours that cut through the heather and trample roots along the way. I mucked through where the damage was already done. Realistically, any time saved by being able to beeline the route was probably used up changing shoes, but it was fun acting more like a kid.

The meadows were pretty. Most of the early flowers were gone, but there was enough color left to please the eye. Purple heather flowers and clumps of little white blossoms had the accompaniment of rich green backdrops of grasses and other foliage. Little watercourses of clear runoff meandered through pocket gardens that landscapers never quite capture.

The water running through the meadow was not the murky swamp water of some lowlands. It was clear and populated with small escaped lake trout. Unfortunately, wetlands are not the place to sit out the winter, so the fish we saw were pleasant to see but probably doomed. That's nature.

From the middle of the meadow, it was possible to get an unobstructed view of Townsend. The ridge looked taller and I appreciated how large the talus fields were. I knew that what looked like knee high plants were eye high bushes and that the thin ground cover was really thick meadows of heather and blueberry.

A bit of a slip and a slog later we crossed the last little stream onto the dry land near the lake's outlet. We picked out the trail to the cabin and soon settled on the porch. My sandaled feet were black with mud. I washed them off in the cold lake water before sitting down for lunch.

The lake looked better than before. Most of the tree pollen was gone. Did it sink or flow downstream? Fish jumped and swallows swooped over the surface. It looked like play, but I know that it was their daily struggle for food and survival. They make it look good and fun though. Winter was finally banished and summer had arrived. The change took very little time and was dramatic. A few months back everything was locked in and blanketed. With the snow gone and the sun high, everything looked alive. Rocks were populated with commuting squirrels and the lake water was rippled with fish. The birds filled in the blanks and the plants covered the rest.

We were alone at the lake. It is refreshing to know that unprotected places like Eagle Lake are not so overrun that a person can't go there for some quiet. All it seems to take is timing and a bit of luck.

We sat on the porch and talked about the rapid growth and changes down in town. What would happen to the lake? The fact that a cabin could exist at Eagle Lake made us wonder about what could happen to unprotected areas. Ironically, we all liked the idea of owning the cabin. That is one of those incredibly common topics of conversation amongst hikers at beautiful spots: "Wouldn't it be great to live in a place like this?" Owning that view, a place to fish, a place to ski, or a fortress of peacefulness, is very alluring. We wouldn't spend all of that effort getting there if we didn't like what was out there. Getting to stay there would make it even better, or at least it feels that way.

Reality is a wonderfully limiting notion. Most places in the wilderness are uninhabitable by today's standards. There's no reasonable way to bring in a road and utilities. Becoming self-sufficient is possible but either expensive or difficult. A business running a resort might manage something, but it was more than we wanted to tackle. Even as a vacation cabin, it was more trouble than it was worth. The upkeep would be expensive. None of us wanted to deal with the vandalism that was ruining it. I tried to imagine the business in real estate if none of the land was designated National Forest or wilderness. There would probably be lots of cabins being battered by nature and vandals. It would be hard to get away from the signs of civilization. We wondered if any organization knew much about the area. Was it a forgotten niche, too far from the pass to be considered wild and too far from town to be considered convenient?

Our opinions didn't really matter and we knew it. We were there for lunch and a view. I left them there after I ate my sandwich. They had been nice enough to let me tag along, but I didn't want to impose and monopolize their day. Besides, we talked so much on the way in that I hadn't taken many pictures and I wanted to capture the early summer.

Pictures should be taken when they are seen. I know that and continue to ignore it. That costs me shots. The lighting can't stay the same. By the time I left the lake, the occasional puffy cloud was replaced with a complete grey overcast and a wind. Wet weather was due the next day and it came to the mountains a bit early.

I learned that wearing the sandals helped me get some good shots. I was a lot less hesitant about getting into the right position because I didn't have to worry about two hundred dollar footwear with heavy lugged soles ripping and trampling the meadow. I took about two dozen shots of flowers, gardens, and even got a few shots of alternate routes on Townsend.

The time passed quickly and soon I was on the far dry side of the meadow. With the clouds in, the wind was up and the bugs were blown away. Except for the lack of sun, it was a pleasant, quiet time in the meadow.

I switched back into my hiking shoes after my feet dried a bit. I knocked most of the dirt off with my socks. Then I put on the dirty socks. Maybe there was a flaw in my plan. Despite the crunchy bits, my feet suddenly felt much warmer wearing socks and shoes. The cold was something I hadn't noticed until it was replaced with warmth. The runoff in the meadow felt warm compared to the lake, but it obviously was chilly enough to numb my toes. Warm boots felt luxurious. Simple pleasures feel the best.

The trail back down wasn't hard to follow. Familiarity helps. I fended off the brush and cobwebs by carrying my hiking stick in front of me. For a while, I rested the tip on the brim of my hat and let the branches ride up and over me. It felt odd, probably looked odder, but worked well.

We had swept the trail of spider webs by walking through a couple of hours earlier, but new ones were strung across the trail as I came back through. They were industrious little buggers.

Much brush swatting later I was back at the car. There was a view back up the valley that showed almost the entire face of Townsend Mountain. It is a long ridge of scree and shrubs capped by a sharp jagged crest. I hadn't noticed the jagged parts before. Approaching it from the back door looked intriguing. Maybe some other time. I wanted to get home and wash my feet.

July 25-27

Friday, July 25

I had seen Barclay when it was quiet and I was alone. Supposedly, that was a rare combination. Guidebooks and friends told me it was usually noisy and crowded. I never experienced it. The only way to see it was to get a front row seat to the show on a gorgeous summer weekend. That was my best chance of meeting the Barclay most folks talked about. There'd probably be families and people roaming about and relaxing in the nice weather. Someone would end up in the water. There was also a very strong chance that some part of the crowd would make me wince. I wanted to see how many people showed up, how noisy it got, and what other people would do there. In my mind, I saw two main groups, the picnickers and the partiers. Would any of them look for the peacefulness and extreme solitude that I found in the middle of the week? What did folks want?

To get a front row seat, I got there in the middle of a Friday morning. That gave the mid-week campers time to pack and empty the best sites. Imagine getting to the lake and playing vulture watching for people to pack and leave. That wouldn't be any fun. It also meant I was there before the Friday night rush. There were four cars at the trailhead, but there were at least eight campsites at the lake. I wasn't too worried.

One of the campers was already out at her car. I assumed she was packing the car to leave. Nope. Her tailgate was her kitchen and she preferred to eat breakfast there. She hiked out to the car rather than have breakfast at camp. After all of that work I would have driven down to the highway and had breakfast at The Baring Store. It was also a regular general store with everything you need, including a post office. The drive wouldn't take much more time and the food was probably better than whatever she cooked up in the back of her car. She was happy enough sitting at the trailhead.

According to her, life at the lake was quiet. She got there Thursday night to make sure she had a spot for the weekend. I wasn't the only one with that goal.

Getting ready was easy. I had no plans to get energetic with my hiking, so I didn't need to change into heavy hiking boots. The weather was forecast to be exceptional, so I left the heavy foul weather gear at home. The tent's rainfly stayed in the car. My jacket was a lightweight fleece with no hood or major rain protection. If the weather got bad, I'd rely on my emergency tarp and a quick hike out to the car for anything else. The stove was my tiniest and the usual cook set was replaced with a teapot and two metal plates. About the only thing as heavy as ever was the food. The essentials barely filled half of my pack. All of that extra space looked too empty, so I bought some high volume, low nutrition fun food that normally doesn't get anywhere near my pack: beer and chips. Everyone has their luxuries and guilty pleasures. Those were mine.

I wasn't in a hurry to get to the lake. I slowly hiked along snapping lots of shots of flowers in bloom, berries bunched on bushes and the most intense lighting I had seen there slicing through the canopy. Big red bursts of elderberries stood out from the ends of branches like offerings to passing wildlife. The berries were like tiny red ball bearings, but together they made a seed head as big as a sweet potato. Evidently, they are not something for hikers to nibble on. They looked pretty though. Along the side of the trail down at ankle level were the tiniest white sprays of flowers. Each blossom was smaller than confetti and stood on stems that looked impossibly thin. Above my head was Devil's Club in its prime. In the last few months, it had gone from shoots sprouting from the ground to thorny stems four feet overhead with club-ish seed heads and flower clusters. The leaves were backlit and glowed. It looked so nice that I almost forgot how much I hated the plant.

The season had been dry. It was bad enough that back at the trailhead were a couple of signs imposing fire restrictions. One was the simplest graphic saying something like, "Campfires prohibited". The other was a two page legalese discourse that said the same thing. The official notice was a surprise. The area almost gets enough rainfall to be a temperate rain forest but evidently things were much drier than usual. A couple little streams flowed across the trail like always and there was one persistent creek flowing through a marshy area as usual, but the forest was quiet. Things are most obvious in their absence. The sound of water flowing in Barclay creek was gone. Before I got to the footbridge, it was obvious that weeks without rain had drained the lake enough to dry out the stream. It was quiet. The streambed was a long swath of dry grey stones meandering through the trees. Last fall it looked a bit like that, but pools of water were left behind then. This time as I crossed the footbridge I was above rocks and downed trees. If someone told me the lake was gone, I could have imagined it. The campfire restrictions were obviously needed.

The threat of forest fires didn't seem to deter the first hikers I saw. Three teenage campers walked along the trail on some errand that involved a hatchet. My eye captured the image, but my brain was reminiscing about being a teenager so the implications of the hatchet didn't register until I was a quarter mile past them. By then I was at the lake and I had no idea where they were. I couldn't stop thinking about what they were up to and what I should, could or would do about it.

The lake level was down ten to twelve feet since my June visit. That is a lot for any lake. The beach was no longer a few feet wide and hiding under the trees. There was enough sand to hold a volleyball game, though it was more than a bit tilted. Lots of the balls would end up in the water. Most of the downed trees that lay in the lake were exposed and abandoned to dry on the shore. A few were webbed with abandoned tangled fishing line. I couldn't walk around the lake in winter, but in summer it looked like everyone could take a lap. The driftwood and foot deep mud would get in the way though.

There was one prime campsite I had in mind. It was about halfway along the lake, had good water nearby and a very good view of Baring. I was very wrong. The lake was so small that the campsite was stranded. Instead of water, it sat beside mud. The lake had lost more than half its length. Seeing the exposed inlet marsh wasn't much of a shock after realizing how much water had left the lake. Camping beside the nice willowy green marsh grass was a possibility, but that was at the price of sitting in mud to filter our drinking water. I wandered back to the last lakeside camp and dropped my pack.

Across the trail from my campsite were a young father and his two sons. They were packing to leave and gave me the rundown on the essentials like bugs and such. He was a nice guy. We commiserated over trivial trail talk and also discussed how and when to chastise hatchet wielding teenage boys. He had some job where he worked with kids and guessed that there was no way to stop them. If their parents hadn't taught them respect of nature and responsible camping during the last few years, there was nothing one of us could do in a short conversation.

I rationalized my inaction by remembering the local forest ranger's problem. Getting anything to burn took great effort. It was so hard to get things to burn that the ranger couldn't practice setting controlled fires. His boss wanted him to practice, but getting a rain forest to burn is a worthless exercise. According to him, the long term danger was much greater because there are very few small burns to keep the fuel from piling up. On the rare occasion when the forest ignites, it has so much fuel and will burn so hot that civilization can't stop it. Mother Nature's rains and snows are the only tools big enough to put out fire of that size. I was a little leery about the hatchet-wielding youngsters' campfires, but kept in mind that the odds were that nothing would happen. At least their fire pit was probably on a sandy beach where it was safest. Not safe, just safest. Sparks fly and they couldn't stop them.

My powers of persuasion are so dismal that trying to convince them to obey the fire regs would probably inspire them to light a bonfire. At times like that, I really wish there was a more active official presence in the woods, or at least a good cell phone signal so I could call for advice. Ah, but budgets and cell phone reception sound easier to fix than they are. Otherwise, the problem would have been solved.

Setting up camp was very easy. The beach was fairly smooth. There were hardly any bugs. I had lots of room to spread out my stuff. About the only hazard was the chipmunk patrol. The little striped furballs were aggressive. Did timidity and wildness vanish on the weekends? Did they count the lean four weekdays waiting for the feast from Friday through Sunday? I hung my food from a branch and scared them away when they got too pesky. I've lost enough food to the little critters in other busy places. Finding chipmunk poop in trail mix taught me to not encourage the wildlife. They are cute, but I draw the line at making friends with something that uses my food as a toilet. Where had they been during those solo overnights of mine? Maybe there was something to them knowing when to visit the lake.

After camp was set and the food secured I walked along the trail to see how many folks were there and if anything else about the lake had changed. One of the luxurious additions was a brand new toilet. I even found a second one at the far end of the lake. That was double the luxury. For those unfamiliar with wilderness toilets, think of an outhouse without the house. A wilderness toilet is frequently a wooden box set over a hole in the ground. The box has a hole in it like a toilet, and it is used for the same activity, but there is nothing to flush and frequently plenty to smell and swat. The bugs like them. It doesn't sound like luxury until you try to perform the same task without the already built box and hole.

Besides that though, the big story was the dryness and the indigenous population. Either a new bird had flown in or some teenagers were really bad at birdcalls. I suspect the latter. I also took some documentary photos of the shoreline. I was so impressed with watching the lake fill over the wet season that I wanted to record its shrinkage. The pictures weren't artistically composed or lit. They were good for showing how much beach, or how little lake, there was. One major difference was that in the winter I didn't have to compose the shot to leave out the half-naked sunbather. She was lying chest down so she was discreet, but I didn't want to look like some old letch snagging shots of partially clad women.

Back at camp, I sat down, cracked a beer, opened the chips, and read a book. That is decadence. The weather was warm and sunny and the sun was high enough to sneak past Baring and hit the beach. At three o'clock, the sun stood right over the peak. The far shore was in shade, but the beach by me was hot.

During the other three seasons, people were much more sociable and polite. As I sat there reading, two people walked within five feet of me without saying hello or pardon me. They were trying to get to a different part of the beach by cutting through the campsite. Maybe they thought it was more polite to not disturb me. Their aloofness didn't bother me, but it pointed out that a weekend in July would be different than a weekday in April. The more people that were there, the less friendly it was. It wasn't like everyone was quietly sneaking by each other to maintain some sense of serenity. I heard lots of random bursts of laughter and shouting from out of the trees, down the beach and across the lake.

I couldn't hear the water flowing into the lake. It is the one sound that was always there. It was possible that the cascading waterfall that fed the lake was dry and quiet, but I suspect its song was drowned out by sounds of people. Nature could take the blame too. A strong wind noisily blew through the trees, but I wasn't going to complain about it. The wind swept the bugs away.

This weekend would be different from my previous trips. It wouldn't be a solo. Eric, a hiking buddy for more than a decade, needed a weekend off, so I invited him along. Usually we are shouldering packs for miles and climbing thousands of feet. Hiking to Barclay would be a big change. He had the nasty habit of working, so he couldn't get there until late Friday afternoon. Add another car to the parking lot. Just for the fun of it, I walked out to the trailhead to meet him and so he'd have someone to hike in with. Besides, it gave me the opportunity to take some more photos.

Sitting in the car waiting for him was more decadence. My mindset had shifted to camping mode, so sitting in a metal vehicle on an upholstered seat was luxurious. To make things better, there was free entertainment. I listened to the radio while I watched the dance of the packing campers. It was an interesting study in people's priorities and comfort zones. Everyone has different essentials and I watched serious gear and frivolous toys go into backpacks. One group had one intrepid adult and four or five young boys. They were religious enough to begin the hike with a prayer. That part was fine with the boys, but they made yucky noises when one of them suggested holding hands while they prayed. The wilderness wasn't as scary as holding another boy's hand.

Eric showed up right on time. I considered that amazing because he had to navigate traffic from south of Seattle in Tukwila to Baring on a Friday night and time it just right. That is an impressive feat. Mastering rush hour traffic is a much more useful skill than anything required for a quiet weekend camping trip.

The sun was close to setting, so we focused on getting to camp, getting settled and making dinner. Good conversation and our usual hiking pace made the trail go by so quickly that we didn't notice much along the way. Eric got a better chipmunk reception than I did. As he walked past a tree on the edge of camp, a cube of bread dropped beside him. It was a gift, though possibly unintentional, from above.

After dinner, a few more campers came in and the dayhikers left. The place didn't get nearly as crowded as I had expected. There were about seven people with fishing poles camped on the exposed peninsula and a few more scattered tents, but there was room for more.

That was before nightfall.

As the sun neared the horizon it lined itself up with the lake and spotlit stands of trees, stumps in the water, ridge lines, and marsh grass. Streaks of light and color cut past deep shadows along Baring's flanks. The forest below Baring was dark green except for a few trees tall enough to catch golden light on their highest branches. It was the same gorgeous light show I watched in June, replayed for the benefit of the crowd. While it showed off and we relaxed watching it, more mundane tasks took place behind us. Over our shoulders, we noticed campsite resettlements in progress. Someone didn't like their first choice and wasted no time picking up their tent and carrying it along the trail. Considering that most tents are almost the size of a queen bed and that he was carrying it over his head, he defined bulky and ungainly. I knew what the brush was like along that bit of trail. I tried killing it months earlier, but it had grown back. If the brush didn't puncture the tent, I would be amazed. We got to watch the light show. They got to rearrange camp. We got the better deal.

We pulled our sleeping bags out of our tent and spread them out on the beach so we could comfortably watch the last of the sunset. Afterwards we talked and switched on headlamps to read. In front of us was a peaceful lake drifting into shadow. Behind us was a serenade of hammers on tent stakes and hatchets in wood. A few frogs joined in. They lacked volume, but they had persistence and population on their side. Eventually Nature made the biggest noise. The only other disruption was the ka-plushing of rocks in water. I know someone who claims that any man near a body of water will feel compelled to throw rocks into it. It is some basic need to either fill up the lake or harass the fish. I don't know that the stone throwers were male. To us they were a covey of headlamps that bobbed by the shoreline in the night and made splashes as they went.

Darkness wasn't enough to stop some folks from hiking in and setting up camp. At about 1AM, after the frogs quit, we heard a group of young women pitching a tent twenty feet behind us. There were giggles, more whacking hammer noises, and no attempt at volume control. At least it sounded like they were enjoying themselves, but it wasn't restful. Well, that was another piece of the picture I wanted to experience. I added it to the list.

As if the strange noises weren't enough to keep us awake, under a clear, starry sky a small band of clouds crept up to a ridge a few miles away and somehow managed to rain on us. It wasn't much and I certainly hope it was rain and not something unpleasant from our neighbors. A few minutes later it stopped, but it kept us up a lot longer as we tried to understand how rain could get from there to us. At least while the neighbors kept us up we passed the time by watching the stars, planets, satellites, and planes go by. It was a brilliant night, but where did that rain come from?

Saturday, July 26

Waking up was easy to do. The dawn light hit Baring full on and reflected back on us. It is hard to sleep with 4,000 feet of bright rock shining on you. The lake was calm and covered in a slowly sliding thin fog that drifted along until it suddenly vanished. A few bugs were about, but the busiest traffic was the local bird population. I guessed that they flew up to the sunlight to warm up. Eric and I looked at each other across the stretch of beach and tried to figure out if we should wait for the bags to catch some sun. Hygiene and hunger got us out of our bags, but not before we added a couple of layers of clothes. Less than ten minutes later the top layer was dumped and before breakfast was over we were back to shirts and shorts.

It was easy enough to wander back to the trailhead for some things we left in our cars in such magnificent weather. Remember the woman eating a tailgate breakfast on Friday? She went back for food. Eric went back for film. I went back for a balaclava. It should have been a short and easy trip, but it was three hours before we were back in camp. The leisurely trip to the trailhead took about an hour and there was a bit of time spent at the car, but the most time was spent on the trip back. We took a major detour at the footbridge. That was definitely the long way home.

When we got to the footbridge and looked at the dry streambed, we decided it would be interesting to use the streambed instead of the trail. We'd never hiked up a dry streambed. Streams, outflows, and creeks in the Cascades are amazing mazes of enormous boulders, giant fallen trees, deep eddy-carved holes, thick moss and foliage. When they are full of water they are beautiful to look at and treacherous to travel in. We had a rare opportunity to see one dryly and safely from its middle and get a feel for the contorted path the water follows. There was no guarantee that we could make it the entire way. One big pool or an impassible tangle of logs could stop us, but it was worth the try. The weather was excellent and at worst we could always get back on the trail at the footbridge.

The streambed looked like a long pile of dry, grey, smooth rocks, but we were surprised to find that there was water. Every hundred yards or so we found little pools. The surprising part was that they weren't stagnant. Water flowed through them slowly, coming out from under one pile of rocks and disappearing under the next set. If we stood still, we could hear the stream moving through the rocks below us. It sounded like it was a few feet down. That was an eerie feeling for two reasons. The first was that we were walking over a stream. The second was that the lake wasn't done draining and was going to continue shrinking. The Puget Sound's dry season is roughly mid-July through Mid-September. With the lake already down about ten feet we originally thought the losses would stop as the lake level got below the outlet. We looked at evidence that the area was porous enough to keep the water flowing and the lake shrinking. Two more months of near drought were not going to help.

Streambeds are filled with rocks worn smooth from the flowing water. Most people know that. Those rocks don't always stay where they are put. The ones we walked on were round and loose. In places, it was like walking on a field of uneven bowling balls that shifted at each step. Walking on them was also noisy. Every step made a clunk or two. We didn't sound, or look, graceful, but that is nothing new.

There was very little open bank or sandy shore. Climbing out was a possible but definitely messy option. Trees and bushes reaching out over the streambed hid most of the bank. They wanted the open space that was over where the water normally was. That was where the sunshine was strongest but they didn't cover it completely. For us it meant we were warm and walking along a pleasant but bumpy and walled-in sunlit path.

The streambed was definitely not a flat straight trail. At changes in direction or elevation, at turns and shelves, the stream piled boulders and logs into mazes that blocked our progress. We got through by splitting up, taking different paths, and calling back and forth until we found a reasonable way through. With the stream at full, the force of the water and the convoluted formations would have made the trip impossible or at least stupidly hazardous. Some boulders were larger than trucks and some logs were a few feet in diameter. They were big enough to treat with respect and were awesome proof of the power of the water.

The obstacles wedged in above our head were large enough to require cranes and floodwater is what put them there.

Finally, we got to the outlet and got to climb the short dry waterfall that few must see when it is flowing at full force. Then it must be powerful, beautiful and dangerous.

We climbed the biggest rock at the outlet and looked up the length of the lake. Below us on the left was a wide sandy area that had been flooded in the spring. It had become the biggest, flattest beach on the lake. From that vantage point, it was obvious that the lake was only half as long as it had been in the winter. As the summer moved along, more people were coming to fish in an ever shrinking pond. Fishing in a barrel wouldn't be much different.

From our vantage point, we could see 25 people and at least ten tents. But there must have been more. There were dayhikers wandering about and campsites that we couldn't see. No wonder the place had two toilets. Peacefulness was gone. The people sounded like kids during recess.

We were back on the beach three hours after we left camp. More tents were up, though some looked like they weren't going to stay that way. They were ready to collapse. Either they were cheap or not put up right. At the unzipped entrance to one were two open bags of potato chips. Anyone for happy chipmunks? The tent behind ours had a car camping stove big enough to cook full racks of ribs. Around their tent were plastic glasses of orange juice. The bottles of wine and the half gallon of tequila we saw on the beach suggested that the OJ wasn't alone in the cups. The giggle and bikini quotient was much higher than on Friday. Were they part of a sorority?

One trio hiked through the midst of the partying crowds looking distinctly out of place. They were dressed for much more serious hiking. For some reason, which was probably evident to everyone else, they came to us for advice. They wanted to hike to Eagle Lake and didn't know the route or the conditions. I had to hold myself back from gushing data at them. The leader was from Germany and his partners were from the Orient. They made an interesting group. Hiking with them would have been fascinating, but I satisfied myself with playing consultant and wishing them well.

For me it was time to take a nap. On earlier hikes it was easy to fall asleep. July was much noisier. Kids were running around or swimming. A couple of dogs were jumping in and out of the water. The bottle fueled party was under way. We heard cans opening and corks popping. A few quiet folks were trying to coax fish onto hooks, but I didn't think there was much hope of that. It was not as noisy as a city park on a sunny day but it was a lot noisier than springtime at Barclay. Eric has two daughters and thought it wasn't noisy at all, but he can probably sleep through a slumber party. It all depends on what you compare it to.

Later in the afternoon, we were rested and restless. We took advantage of the lowered waterline and the exposed beach to walk around the lake.

Our walk started on the sandy beach but that only lasted until we got to the outlet. There, a pile of weathered logs formed a standing obstacle course that I remembered as a floating maze two months earlier. The logs were stacked into a raw timber climbing course that was almost stable. Mom Nature builds her playground equipment with very big pieces of wood but doesn't use nails or glue.

Getting past the logs also got us past all the campers. We were under the shadow of Baring, where the beach was more of a terraced rocky shelf than a sandy shore. Camping there would be like trying to sleep on a sloped pile of baseballs. The shore was much steeper than the campsite side of the lake and only about half as wide. We thought about getting off the unsteady rocks but the border between the beach and the forest was an abrupt little wall topped with thick tangled undergrowth. There was no sign that anyone ever made a trail through there. We stayed on the beach.

Finally getting to that other side of the lake gave me my first view of the ridge opposite Baring: the Barclay side of Merchant peak. The trees in camp were thick enough to block the view of what was up there, so I hadn't seen that hillside very often. The peak and ridge were imposing and formidable. In comparison to Baring, they were merely steep and rocky, but the land was tough enough to cancel thoughts of hikes or quick bushwhacked climbs. The ridge and the land below it were like Townsend Mountain, long, wide, open and steep, but the crags on the ridge were more severe and the slopes below were broken up by a lot more rocky outcrops. The base of the ridge was close enough to the shoreline of Barclay that I wondered if some of the nighttime rockfalls I heard earlier were from Merchant instead of Baring. Both were steep enough and had evidence of recent slides. If rocks fell from Merchant, then the campsite at Barclay didn't seem as safe as it did before. Ignorance was bliss.

Eventually the rocky shore met the broad mud flats that surrounded the inlet. The sand, rocks, and logs were replaced with mud and grass. Instead of guarding against twisted ankles, we concentrated on staying out of boot sucking mud holes. The grass looked healthy and deep. Evidently, it was adapted to large changes in the lake level. Maybe that happens often. Nearer the water though, the land was an expanse of mud. Nothing lived there, so maybe the lake was lower than usual.

For the five young boys around a stranded ten foot puddle, the low lake level was a treat. They had their own mud hole to play with. They threw mud at each other. They belly flopped into a mud wash. They threw mud at the mud. We had no clue what they or their clothes really looked like. Sitting safely back from the mess was one relaxed and attentive adult. This was a wise man. He stayed clear. It was five kids and a mud tub. We steered around them and enjoyed the show. Norman Rockwell would do them just right.

That was enough effort for us. We got back to camp for some snacks and relaxation. Eric set up his hammock. I crashed in the tent.

Different animals seemed to handle the chaos differently. The few bugs about had more targets. The chipmunks were better fed. On the downside were the birds that had fewer safe places to sit. There were few large birds and I saw no evidence of wild mammals larger than a squirrel. The trees and shrubs couldn't escape, but despite the chopping sounds and the smell of wood smoke, there seemed to be very little destruction. Temperatures in the eighties meant less of a need for fires. The fish were more harassed than hooked, though that wasn't a surprise. At busy lakes, the fish outsmart the anglers. As disruptive as we are as a species, we probably weren't as much of a nuisance as the low water level.

There was a certain lawlessness at the lake. The unwritten and strict laws of survival, the official laws of government, and the cultural laws of society all affect our lives. In the high country miles from anyone, the laws of survival are paramount. In town people worry about what the police and their friends will think. Places like Barclay Lake sit between the extremes where things relax. Surviving a July night at Barclay Lake simply means not doing anything stupid. The police aren't going to drop by, and you can leave behind those people whose rules bug you the most. That kind of lawlessness is useful. Society and people need relief valves. I realized that the weekend crowd was there for relief. I felt it too.

Usually I head into the backcountry and go on solo hikes to see nature and get reminded of the laws of survival. My life becomes clearer when I get to see the world the way it was without humans, and where I have to provide for myself instead of relying on public water, sewage systems, and pizza delivery. When I get back home, I am much more appreciative of tap water and flush toilets. The people crowding the lake with big gas grills and half-gallon bottles of tequila weren't there to celebrate nature. They were there to feel free. Done right, that is healthy and something valuable to our society. Done wrong and it becomes an example of why our species is not ready for life under anarchy. Some folks were fine examples for the need for strong governance. Of course, no one thought they were doing anything wrong. Most of them weren't even thinking. They simply wanted to have fun.

There was definitely a different point of view there that I never recognized before. Instead of trying to get to somewhere like a lot of backcountry hikers, a lot of the folks at Barclay were trying to get away from somewhere. They weren't as interested in looking at the view as they were in forgetting their normal life in town. Barclay was remote enough and close enough that they could get away from their normal life and manage to bring along their luxuries. They probably saw their time there as a hardship, and as a rough but welcome change of pace. Eric and I saw luxury. The tents and stoves were bigger. The gear was much cushier. There was no concern about tomorrow's weather. Unfortunately, there was more trash and the noises were louder. They scared off the birds for a weekend. That wasn't great for the birds, but it is a worthwhile trade if the birds recover and folks are more agreeable when they get back home.

I've thought about resorts at places like Barclay. I wouldn't invest in a building sitting in the path of boulders from Baring and Merchant, but mountain resorts do well and are much more common in other states and countries. The hiking in Austria is remarkable that way. But a resort would have rules. Making Barclay protected wilderness would also have rules. The way I saw it there were rules, but most were ignored and unenforced, so effectively they don't exist. I will admit that it was nice to see that some places exist where the rules are a little bit looser. I can hope that people don't abuse the privilege, but it is inevitable that someone will do something stupid. It is a bit of that freedom that our country is known for. For me, I am more comfortable following the rules, and safely camping there on quiet weekdays.

By the end of the day, we witnessed a fleet of rafts. Two inflatables cruised the lake. Sometimes they were driven by oars. Sometimes people floated around in them and used their arms as paddles. One drifted by and looked empty. Another trolled by without a care about catching anything besides a tan. Three kids tried straddling a floating log and swimming it somewhere, anywhere. Any progress would have been a success. Actually, it seemed like every time they fell off it was a success. It must have been because they had a grand time whenever it rolled over and dumped them. Late in the afternoon after they beached it, one dad even built an outrigger for it. The evening's entertainment was to see if three boys with oars could stay on it long enough, and paddle well enough, to not get blown down the lake. It took them about an hour to realize that when they took a break they lost ground to the wind. Did that mean they steered for shore, set anchor, or gave up and swam back? Of course not. That wouldn't be fun. For about two hours, they paddled the length of Barclay. Walking the shore would have taken twenty minutes, but efficiency wasn't the point.

They weren't the last craft to leave the water. One raft with a persistent fly fisherman floated by as the day got dark. We never saw him catch anything.

The five mud buffalo from the mud puddle came by our spot on the beach. Their guardian coaxed them all into the water. His goal was to get most of the mud off them. Unfortunately, he mentioned that; otherwise, they probably would have jumped in for the fun of it. Because it was his idea, they mumbled and griped. A few minutes later, they forgot that he had anything to do with it. The bunch of them were splashing, shouting, and having a blast. I never noticed if they got much cleaner. They probably slept well that night.

We thought that the day was almost done. All that was left was dinner, drinks and reading. We were settled in with our books and our sleeping bags. We didn't expect quiet, but that was okay.

Then we heard cheering. There was a huge ripping noise that sounded like an old rotten stump getting pushed over. That ticked me off. A bit of lawlessness is fine, but vandalism is going too far. We heard the noise again and I realized that I was wrong and that my self-righteousness should take a break and have a beer. Eric noticed a parachute landing near the outlet. When we heard the noise a third time we followed everyone's pointing fingers and looked up to see a parachute gliding down from Baring. An hour or two earlier we had talked about the nut cases that do things like base jumping and wondered if anyone had tried it from Baring. The face is near to vertical, but neither of us jumps off cliffs so we didn't know if it was possible to base jump a peak like that. The ripping noise that startled us was the parachute opening. No wonder it didn't sound familiar. Evidently, base jumping from Baring was possible.

Those folks had to be tired. The amazing feat of jumping from Baring had to be preceded by the tough task of carrying themselves and their gear up 4,000 feet to the peak. There are incredible people out there. As a matter of fact, there were at least five incredible people out there. A total of five people jumped and made it down safely. The climb must have taken hours and then they seemed to have waited until dusk for the wind to die down. None of them spent much time getting fancy with aerobatics and such though one had smoke. They landed in the big sandy area by the outlet. That must have been some tight maneuvering. I wondered if they couldn't have made it around the mountain and landed down by US2. If so, they would have enjoyed a longer ride as they got to play with the extra 1,800 foot drop in elevation. Maybe that would have been illegal. Legal or not, that was an amazing and unexpected dinner show. It was fun to watch. Some of the kids at the opposite end of the lake felt left out. We could hear them hollering to the jumpers to land over by them. They wanted a piece of the action.

Getting back to the topic of lawlessness and the need for a release, I don't want to know the law about this one. I am simply glad they had a good time and were safe. Besides, is there any legal argument that would work against someone that is willing to throw their body off a 4,000 foot precipice? Forget the laws of society. They were willing to challenge the laws of gravity and that is ruled over by a judge that delivers the swiftest judgment and penalty and does not allow appeals. Amazing. It sure looked sweet and there is no way I am doing that.

Relaxing took a bit more effort after such an incredible show. Nature continued and that has an amazing calming effect. The sun went down. The birds and bats chased the bugs. The chipmunks scurried for scraps. Our edge of the lake got quieter. I think the party moved to the parachutes.

The night was peaceful. There were no midnight hikers trying to erect tents by flashlights and giggles. A bat swooped by. I accidentally folded my sleeping pad right under my hips and had one of the best nights sleeping in a long time. The stars came out and I tracked the night by glimpses of one large orange star that was probably Mars. Whenever I opened my eyes, that small bright dot was farther across the sky until it was lost behind Baring.

Sunday, July 27

Eventually the sky lightened. At first, I thought it was because my eyes had adjusted to the darkness, but the stars were gone. It was time to look for the first light on the mountain. Faces of Baring that never see the sun in the winter are lit for a few hours each cloudless morning in the summer. All of their snow was gone and the clean rock showed patches of lichen and streaks of ores. The shadow of the ridge retreating down the mountain leaving early morning sunshine was a pretty and quiet show to watch from my sleeping bag. The only trick was keeping my eyes open. I tended to drift off long enough that when I opened my eyes more of the mountain was lit. I woke from the last nap of the morning to see Baring as one large orange tinted rock.

Then it was time for the morning game of guessing the best time to get out of the sleeping bag. We weren't the first ones up. The fly fisherman had drifted by in the inflatable raft before the sunlight was halfway down the mountain. I never saw him catch anything, but maybe he didn't care about nibbles and strikes. The first dayhikers were at the lake by 8AM. Certain tents probably wouldn't unzip for hours to come. We knew we had a short hike out, so we leisurely ate breakfast while we packed some things and set others out to dry. Within a couple of hours, everything was dry and packed and we were on the trail.

The trip out was quick. We got to the trailhead before lunchtime. Concentrating on good conversation meant we missed most of the sights along the trail. We couldn't ignore the other people hiking in. We must be people people. On the way out, we met two families headed in towards the lake. At the trailhead, we saw a couple more cars drive up. One car carried a solo hiker who cautiously revealed her embarrassment at going on such an easy hike. For years, she avoided it because it was low, flat and short. That sounded familiar and we knew how she felt. So many times we feel that the best hikes are high, long and hard. That is where the best workouts and greatest solitude are, but it isn't always necessary to suffer to enjoy views of nature. It is a guilty pleasure. Six more cars passed us before we got to the highway. Barclay was going to have a busy day.

Through most of my visits, I noticed a heron that fished the pond at the bottom of the hill. It usually stood there waiting and snapping at fish. Most of the year it patiently waited until the cars went past and then resumed its fishing. It didn't mind when I parked and sat still so I got in the habit of visiting it on my way out. I pulled off the road to wait for Eric to catch up. He'd stopped up above to let some traffic get through a narrow spot. I sat there and watched the heron spook every time a car passed by. There was never a long enough gap between cars for it to settle down to hunt. It had probably seen it all before and learned to cope, but I can't believe that it liked it.

One loud weekend at Barclay was enough for me. The August trip should be another quiet mid-week overnight. Besides, what could more amazing than watching five base jumpers fly off Baring at sunset? No other weekend trip could beat that for energetic entertainment.

August

Tuesday, August 12

Those base jumpers in July kept coming to mind. My curiosity blew away my plans for a quiet weekday overnight. I wanted to climb Baring and see what they had to deal with. Getting themselves and their gear up there could not have been easy. It wasn't like I hadn't considered climbing it before that, but they definitely upped my interest level. I'd finally heard enough personal accounts of folks who had climbed Baring that I decided it was something I should try.

The big run of dry hot weather we had in July vanished in the middle of August. That is rare. The sunshine usually stays until mid-September and browns everything in the meantime. Instead of eighty degree days, it was only in the fifties at the trailhead. The clouds remained from a week of light rain peppered with thunderstorms. The plants and the dirt greedily held on to the new moisture. On the drive to the trailhead, the dust was gone. My tires didn't kick up the usual cloud behind the car and the plants along the road looked much greener. Their new growth sprouted lines of green that encroached from both sides of the road. Some of the side roads were only noticeable because I knew to look for them. The undergrowth was eating them.

It was very early on a Tuesday morning. The early start gave me time to climb. The climb up Baring is about 4,000 feet. Keep in mind that when I say climb I mean steep hiking at most. My feet do almost all of the work. True climbing with ropes, hardware, exposure and the continual threat of death is something for people with half my age and a feeling of invulnerability. I typically manage 1,000 feet an hour so I planned on four or five hours to get up there, time for lunch, and four hours to return. My knees always vote for a descent that is almost as slow as the ascent. Welcome to middle age.

The clouds were moving, but neither my experience nor the forecast gave much hope that they would vanish. As each moved up the valley, another followed it. The ridges were hidden by mists. There wasn't much hope of a view from the summit, but being an optimist, I thought the clouds might part long enough for a view when I got there. It was August, and Washington skies are supposed to be clear for the tourists. A view of the horizon would be great, but I'd be happy enough with a clear view of Barclay.

I was surprised that, except for me, the trailhead was empty. Did the rain scare everyone away?

In the spring, my walk up to the start of the route involved maneuvering around trunks of slide alder. In August, the alder was in full leaf and the branches filled the remaining space. My clothes were wet within fifty feet of wrestling through the shrubbery. The remaining rain or the morning dew clung to me as I shoved back each branch. I found a small clearing and changed into my rain gear. It was as bad as being caught in a steady rain.

The abandoned road leads to some destination that I've never investigated. It was probably a road that went as far as possible to get out the most logs. I stopped at the cairn that marked the beginning of the totally unofficial trail up Baring. It was an impressive cairn standing about three feet high. Moss grew on it so thickly that looked like it had been there for decades. It was a sentinel that watched the climbers go by.

The route takes a turn straight up the hill from the cairn. There are no switchbacks or other trail markers. A muddy hillside beside a stream has been beaten into a crumbling mess that only humans could produce. This was definitely hand and foot hiking and messy. The footing was tenuous. Each step kicked dirt down and my foot slid a bit with it. My hands stabilized me while my feet searched for the next little hint of a foundation. Four thousand feet of that would be an ugly chore and a challenge coming back down.

In the spring I previewed the route, so I knew to bring along gardening gloves. They are hardly standard issue in the backpacking stores, but they helped me concentrate on a getting a firm grip. Otherwise, each handhold takes longer as I check it for thorns and spiders. Most hiking gloves are for protection from rain, wind, and snow, not mud. Gardening clothes can take a lot more punishment and are a lot cheaper.

Above the mud, the path eased a bit as it maneuvered over the rocks and crossed the stream. It became more like a step-less staircase instead of a rung-less ladder. The moisture made it slippery, which is normal for hiking, but it was a bit scary on tilted land.

On the other side of the stream, I hoped to find firmer soil and a more definite track. The route is well enough established to produce that impressive cairn, but the traffic must not be great enough to build a boot beaten path. The route was a series of alternating boot-sized indentations in a mix of crumbling soil, fallen leaves, and needles. The grade barely lessened and I was sweating. At least it looked like I would be out of the brush for a while, so I found a stable place to stand on while I stuffed my jacket and rain pants into my pack. Getting rid of the outer layer of plastic made it easier to reach for handholds or pull my leg up onto tree roots.

The footsteps wove a brown path up around the tree trunks and low leafless branches. The route was bordered by two drainages filled with tumbling green swathes of Devil's Club and elderberry. There wasn't any underbrush to deal with along the path, but I wanted eye protection from the dead branches that stuck out in every direction.

It was a grunt, but I can do that. Following a route like that is the simple but grueling task of watching for leftover footsteps and grinding my way along them. I am not trained as a tracker, but I definitely have gotten better at finding the human wear patterns in the forest. Every step we take leaves a mark. I doubt that I could follow a person who was trying to evade me, but it becomes much easier trying to trace where dozens or hundreds of people have traveled. Get enough people walking somewhere, and the dirt gets turned or packed and the trees scuffed enough that it is obvious that people have been by.

The route finding wasn't as easy as I expected. It seemed like a route that would be popular enough to attract lots of the aggressive types because of its destination. Instead of a well-beaten path, the footsteps were in dirt so loose and on a slope so steep, that the dirt fell away and took the trail signs with it. Rather than packing down, the ground held an impression for a while, but crumbled with a slight extra shove from the toe of my boot. The forest was also thick enough to rain down fresh needles over tracks that were probably only days old. Any established footprints were probably covered quickly.

I lost the trail. That happens often enough when I bushwhack that it didn't bother me. I don't panic. I couldn't see the trail above me, so I looked below me. I could see my ridiculously clear path that led right to my feet. The slope was steep enough that it was hard to see the uphill footprints because most of them were at or above eye level. Looking down though, it was easy to see where my boots kicked away the top layer of needles and left dark brown earth. The path down was obvious. The path up was hidden. A couple of minutes of extrapolating from my previous path and squinting at smudges above me and I guessed which way to go next.

The weather did not help. Gaps in the trees showed the sea of clouds that washed through the valley. The clouds and trees were thick enough that I was in deep shade. The tree canopy alone was thick enough to keep out most of the light; otherwise, the green borders would happily sneak towards each other. They were kept at bay by the lack of light.

Amidst my griping and climbing, I came across evidence of serious human traffic. What I was doing was recreational. Someone had been there with a chainsaw. Either loggers or fire crews had been there. I climbed over old cleanly cut stumps and charred logs. Lumberjacks and firefighters are known to be stout folks, but I was overwhelmed when I realized how much effort they went to. I had trouble getting to that spot. They had to do it in work gear while carrying chainsaws. It is easy to take for granted how much work goes into providing wood for furniture or in stopping fires from getting out of control. My comfort level was being challenged. What they did was much more dangerous. They probably weren't trying to go straight up to the top like me, but I was impressed with what they accomplished.

I got lost again. I found my way again. I got lost again. I found my way again. I lost track of how often that happened. Each time I'd look up the hill for evidence. I'd look down the hill and guess where the path headed. If that didn't work, I checked about ten or twenty feet on either side of some landmark that I couldn't lose. One time I climbed up a bit, looked down the hill to see the path, and then maneuvered over to rejoin it.

The hillside was steep and close to the edge of my comfort zone. I knew that for me, safely climbing up is easier than safely climbing down. On the way down it is too easy to slide. My comfort zone was also challenged by the time it took for route finding. I didn't know how fast I was gaining elevation, but I knew that looking for the route was taking as much time as climbing it. I started to doubt the safety of climbing back down through the maze. After summiting, it would be particularly difficult because I would be tired.

I've managed to scale small rock outcrops on lots of hikes, but I found an obstacle that stymied me. The path seemed to go up through a gap between two trunks of a tree. On the downhill side of the tree, the slope was very steep and the ground was very loose. The next step up was at about chest height. Between that loose footing and the possible handholds on the trunk were a couple of roots that looked like they'd been used as steps. When I tried to get close enough to use them, the ground slid out from under my foot. I could get my foot high enough if I pulled up on the trunks, but the root wobbled when I gave it any of my weight. For minutes, I stood below this crux realizing what it would take to make that next bit of progress. It would take commitment. I would have to commit my weight to the pull-up, trust the roots to stay in place and count on my hands to not slip on wet bark. I would also be committed to getting myself back through that point.

My doubts were obviously too great and probably overblown. Climbing without confidence is dangerous. Maybe it is my age, but I am much more aware of what drives me. I wanted to climb Baring. Climbing Baring would be an accomplishment that I remembered every time I drove along Highway 2. One of the most enjoyable things about hiking for me is getting to the top of some peak and sucking in a 360 degree view. I loved getting to that one high point on Townsend. I won't forget that. I also knew that I didn't want to be the subject of Search and Rescue. Besides the embarrassment, it costs a lot. Whether it's money directly out of my pocket or indirectly through taxes, I didn't see my enjoyment of the climb outweighing the impact a failure would have on others. Every search and rescue kicks off disturbances in dozens of lives. When that happens to save someone from a disaster, it is noble and the very sort of thing that we should do for each other. It was silly to risk that possibility when the view from the summit was likely to be of the inside of a cloud. It came down to this: I wanted to climb Baring, but I didn't need to climb Baring. At least for that day, the risk was greater than the benefit.

Turning back wasn't easy emotionally. I felt like I failed. Either my climbing or route finding skills weren't good enough for the task. An act of prudence is responsible, but rarely makes the day more fun. Prudence does however mean there will probably be many more days to enjoy. The mountain wasn't falling down fast enough to vanish in my lifetime. I knew I could go back and climb it when the conditions were better and maybe even do it with friends along for fun, help, and support.

Climbing down wasn't easy physically either. Following my footprints down was easier than figuring out how to climb up, but somewhere I got lost again. It was not my day for bushwhacking. I knew things were bad when I had to manage my way through Devil's Club. I picked my way back towards the middle of the steep clearing and was glad to find the path again. The only other change in my route was intentional. That muddy slope at the bottom looked like the mudslide in *Romancing the Stone*, but without the attractive actress or a soft place to land. Instead, I stepped into the streambed. It was wet from the mist, but it didn't have too much flowing water. The slightly moist rocks were less slippery than the muddy path.

Walking back down the abandoned road I didn't even put on the rain gear. The car was close enough that I wasn't worried about a little bit of water.

I was only gone for ninety minutes, but I was beat. I am much more impressed with those base jumpers than I was before. I also think they had a good idea about finding some other way down. Floating through the air seems much nicer than grubbing through dirt at each step for hours on end. It is a pity that base jumping involves hauling a hurking big pack up the hill, trusting fabric, a big enough jump to miss the rocks, and a safe landing. People do amazing things for fun.

The more I think about it the more I am convinced that I lost the trail. It had to be easier to follow than where I went.

My curiosity is hard to kill. I could have gone home but there was plenty of day left to play with. I wondered about the lake. Did the rain help refill it or was the water falling through the bottom leaving only mud behind? The clouds lifted enough to let more light in, but the ridges remained hidden. I took a break before taking on the more leisurely task of hiking in to Barclay.

The clusters of small elderberries were redder than before. Other bushes were already spreading their seeds. The season was changing. Little dried seed heads on long stalks poked out into the trail. They lost their seeds when I brushed against them. The birds seemed happy. Maybe it was feast time for them. I noticed at least three birdsongs that were new to me. It is not that I am able to identify birds by their cries, but there are songs that are familiar. It can be difficult seeing the birds making the sound, so I don't try very hard. I was happy enough listening to their music as I hiked along.

The rain ended one of the driest spells of summer. The ground was wet. So were the bushes, but I was back on an established, maintained trail so it wasn't a problem. That change was welcome, dramatic and appreciated after bushwhacking up Baring. My hands didn't have to grasp for tree roots and I didn't have to think about which way to go and how to get back. Instead, my hands were free to give the camera a workout. My mind relaxed.

The fall foliage hadn't turned yet, but there was color from other corners. Big thrusts of orange fungi sprouted from decaying logs in hand sized fans. One colony of them was inside a stump, as if they were hiding. The small red berries I saw last winter grew from bunchberry bushes. The bushes are more a ground cover than a bush. Did those berries survive the winter because no creature wanted them? There were far more of them than I saw in the winter. In various patches, the ground was polka dotted with red.

A bit of mud on the trail was not an issue after my bushwhacking, but I wasn't eager to slip my way along the boardwalks. Sure enough, they were slick. Gripe, gripe, gripe. Walking very slowly kept me from sliding off into the bushes.

I realized that the wildlife might be easier to come across with no one else on the trail. Last month, Eric inadvertently spooked a black bear cub as he drove to the trailhead. I heard a short, loud noise behind me. The boardwalks are noisy, so I stopped and listened. Nothing happened for a couple of minutes, so I turned and started to walk. Then I heard it again. It was from off the trail and about fifty to a hundred feet back. First a thunk and then silence. I've encountered bears with cubs before, so I didn't spook, but I became much more aware. I saw what made the noise as I turned the corner. A little blur of fur ducked under the boardwalk and a pinecone rolled off into the ferns. The thunks I heard were big solid pinecones hitting the ground after a hundred foot fall. They were actually fir cones, not pinecones. Pines' cones have that open look with all the wooden petals opened. Cones from fir trees are solid and heavy. They are more like unbaked potatoes hurtling through the branches. I had been worried about bears, but in some ways the cones were more dangerous. Pinecones don't even know they are attacking and are quiet as they approach at high speed. Bears actively avoid us. I thought about the hardhats we wore on the trail maintenance crew and wished I was wearing one. That blur of fur was some chipmunk or squirrel using the boardwalk as a dining room table. I had interrupted its lunch. Every thirty feet or so was a pile of disassembled pinecone. It was harvest and feast time.

Rain hadn't changed Barclay Creek. As far as it was concerned, the drought continued. It looked as dry as when we hiked up it in July. What happened to the otters?

After the footbridge, the rest of the way to the lake was as green as ever. That stretch never had many berry bushes or flowers. It was more of an evergreen green. The colorful plants all seemed to be on the trailhead side of the stream.

The mushrooms proved me wrong. I spotted a three foot long collection of the broad orange fans spreading out along a log that was between the trail and the lake. They looked like some very natural centerpiece on a very earthy dining room table. I wandered off the trail to look at them and was impressed. They were the same sort that I'd seen earlier on the trail, but these ones were in the open and pointed up. They were hard to miss.

The mushrooms were halfway between the trail and the lake, so rather than go back to the trail I continued and wandered through the underbrush along a fisherman's path. It led to the outlet, but a fisherman using that path would have been disappointed. There were no fish at the end of the path. There was no water at the end of the path. The land was exposed in July. In August, the lake level was down by about another two feet. That meant the beach was wider by about six feet. At the outlet, all of the logs were high and drying. The water barely touched the exposed rocks that held up the logs. The shoreline was black and grey mud pocked with deep holes shaped like human feet.

The clouds obscured the ridges, but surrendered the sky above the valley. I found a rock facing the sun. There was a notch in the rock sized just right for a comfortable recliner. The boulder had a shelf for my lunch and a good headrest. It felt good to sit there drying off, warming up and nodding off. I closed my eyes and enjoyed the quiet.

I don't know how long I was there. That's the way the best naps work. I woke to hear random small splashing sounds. A little grey bird was bobbing its way along the shoreline. I think it was diving for insects, but I can't be sure. It acted like a duck, but swam along without webbed feet. It was a strange skittish little bird. It cruised around the end of the lake diving occasionally and sometimes walking along the shore. It almost looked lost and definitely looked ditzy enough to be having an identity crisis. I never saw it eat anything, but it seemed content as long as I didn't move or make a sound. I got a nap and a floor show.

With lunch in me and a rest behind me, I decided to walk along the beach to where we camped in July. I remembered that part of the beach very well, so it would be easy to tell how much the lake level had fallen. My guess of about an extra two feet was close enough. Navigating around the fallen tree by our old site was easy. Instead of having to climb over it, it was easier to walk around its lower end down by the lakeshore. Lots of footprints had beaten a firm path into the mud.

Other folks had camped there. Enough abandoned fire rings were scattered around that there must have been a lot more crowded weekends since we were there. There were too many of them and they were too close together for anyone to sleep between them if the fires were all burning at once. My guess was that each one was a different camp on a different night. Why didn't they reuse the old fire rings? They probably felt that was cheating. Most of them were built safely. I base that conclusion on the simple fact that the forest hadn't caught fire. That was a lot of risk to take. They were illegal for a reason that season. The fire hazard was extreme. If the forest caught fire, the campers would have a tough race to the cars. Besides, who needs a fire in August? I know. It was something they wanted to do, or thought they were supposed to do. I know people who assume that is what camping is all about: the fire at night. They think it is odd that I haven't lit a campfire in over a decade. No fire means no rummaging around collecting firewood, making kindling, carrying a hatchet, cursing the matches, and smelling like smoke. After sunset, I like to quietly sit still, listen to the forest, and watch the stars on clear nights.

I was surprised to see a familiar piece of driftwood. The outrigger raft was intact and beached on the opposite shore. It looked as crude as ever and would probably stay that way. The raft was put together with nylon that will take a long time to degrade. Getting over to it was not easy. The exposed marsh was solidifying but had tricky soft spots. There were cracks in the mud, but it was also obvious that some footprints postholed into the mud past boot height. I gingerly made my way to the raft. The raft was in good shape considering how quickly it had been built and how roughly it had been used.

On my tour of the shore, I came across another surprise: stumps. Stumps aren't fascinating on their own, but those ones intrigued me because of where they were. They were so far beyond the winter shoreline and so short that they were only exposed when the lake was drastically low. My guess was that it wasn't very long ago that the lake was much shallower and smaller. The trunks were more than a foot in diameter and hadn't decayed much. How long has the lake been the size I came to think was normal? I knew that the rock I napped on fell from Baring, but I originally assumed that the lake was formed by one large rockfall millennia ago. Maybe more falls were involved and each changed the size and shape of the lake. Nature is much more dynamic than is apparent from one visit or even from a year of visits. The implications fascinated me. I realized that the lake I knew might be very temporary geologically and could change easily.

Right after I was thinking geologically, I noticed the frogs in the swamp grass. I think the tadpoles of July grew up, just not very much.

That is also one of the things that fascinate me about hiking. While looking at the stumps and thinking about the geology and history over the decades, right beside it was a small soft fragile creature that might live less than a year. Geology and biology are that close. At night, throw in astronomy. Throw in the crowds and there is sociology. There is a lot for an active mind to think about. At one small lake, there were great examples of the extremes of time, size, and life. The rocks were millions of years old and backed by stars that were billions of years old. Beside the rocks were insects and frogs that may not see an entire year go by, but the trees would be around for centuries. The rocks and stars are enormous, but it is the little frog that gets around the most. We humans are in the middle: which is a good place to watch the ends from.

It was late morning and the lake was all mine, but it was time for me to head home. The early start without a full night's sleep made it a long day. I considered another nap on the beach, but the wind picked up and sent a chill through me. Just to taunt me the clouds thinned enough for me to catch a glimpse of the summit of Baring. On my original schedule, I might have summited about then. Maybe I would have had some views when I got to the top. Or, I could take it as a hint that while climbing the weather was dark and dreary, and while sitting by the lake the weather was warmer and more pleasant. That day I was meant to sit on the beach and relax, not climb and sweat.

In either case, I decided to walk back along the trail instead of the shoreline. One of the consequences of being the first person along a trail is spider webs in the face. Busy trails late in the day are usually clear of spider webs, but an empty trail in a lush area will be strung with enough webs come morning to keep a hiker's hands busy. A web right across the eyes doesn't hurt, but it is at least an annoyance and is definitely a distraction. After I brush away the web, I always wonder where the spider went. Did I acquire a passenger and is it inside or outside my shirt?

At noon, the shaded bushes had not gotten rid of the drops of water on their leaves. The sun shone through in patches though, and when it did, the drops caught the light and looked like shining little glass beads improbably stuck to the leaves. I mourned the death of my old film camera that could catch shots like that. I did the best I could with the digital.

Finally, I met some folks on the trail. Three young men wearing fireman blue uniforms and portable two-way radios purposely hiked their way along the trail. I couldn't think of any fires burning and didn't try to distract them. If there was a fire, I was already headed in the right direction. Ten minutes later, there was an overnight group of four. I told them about the lowered lake level. One of them proudly pointed out to me that he already knew about that from the web. I didn't take credit for my report. There was no reason to challenge his lofty position of expert, even if I was the one who produced the report he found. Near the trail-head, I came across two more parties. They were families up for a dayhike. They might not make it to the lake, but they'd probably have the best time of the lot. Evidently, I left at about the right time.

I was tired. Two hikes in one morning were more than I planned, but I was glad I did it. I was glad I tried, and I was pleased with my prudence. I was also glad to have some private time at the lake.

After eleven months of hiking to Barclay I'd become very familiar with the trail. One more visit and it will be time to introduce myself to a new spot for the next twelve months. My next trip would be to spend a couple of days quietly sitting there, relaxing, and reflecting. I looked forward to it.

September

Sunday, September 7

The best-laid plans go astray, so I shouldn't be surprised that my plans for my final visit got totally lost. The twelfth visit to Barclay was supposed to be a time that gave me a feeling of accomplishment and completion. I wanted to celebrate by camping there for a few nights so I could explore a few niches and remember lots of good times. That sounded nice, but it meant nothing to the thug that broke into my car. Over two thousand dollars worth of hiking gear was gone. Who else in the world can use the kind of odd and archaic equipment that I use? Size thirteen three-pin leather telemark boots are great for what I do, but who else cares? Of course, it doesn't matter who else cares. They were hunting for anything portable. My planned overnight vanished with the loss of my hiking boots, raingear and emergency equipment. The cost was bad enough, but it was going to take me a long time to get the car repaired, find replacement gear and fill out police and insurance forms.

After an initial slug of bureaucracy, I decided to not let the bad guys win. If I couldn't do an overnight, I could at least get a dayhike in. The crooks could slow me down but they wouldn't stop me.

The ever-draining lake was finally going to get a chance to refill. The forecast showed real rain, not just showers. Seattle had just set a record for the longest number of days above seventy degrees. Most of that was without rain. I knew that it would take months for the lake to fill. At least I could be there as the first few drops began the task.

Kaye wanted to see the lake that I had been visiting. Of course, her hiking boots were stolen too, so she was in running shoes. I was lucky enough to have a pair of low-top lightweight hikers at home.

We got a late start. The previous night's party probably had something to do with our sleeping in. If we got lucky, we wouldn't have to worry about parking very far from the trailhead.

Big crowds of cars happened on the summer weekends, but the passage of Labor Day and the forecast for rain were probably the biggest reasons why the trailhead only had six cars in it. In twelve months, I had only seen the parking lot get crowded twice. So much for it being a crowded lake.

It was the kind of day where clouds and sunshine jostle each other. As we got out of the car, the clouds were winning. All of the local peaks were hidden behind moving curtains while the middle of the valley was a mix of low clouds and views of the opposite hillside. There didn't seem to be any imminent rain, which was a good thing because they took my favorite rain jacket too. Kaye was glad it was gone. It was bright orange, dirty and old. I liked it. Our best rain protection was to hope for a large enough weather window for one more dry hike.

On the trail, it was apparent that the first rains had already passed through. The leaves were moist and shiny. Our pants got a little damp if we brushed against a bush. Little drops fell from the trees as the wind lightly swept through. The wet leaves didn't slow us down. The moisture was merely a nuisance. The foliage slowed us down because it looked wonderful. Bright bunchberries surrounded by rich, wet, green leaves meant I spent time taking photos. Even without a camera, the spotlit displays of fattened moss, or the remaining blossoms of something I call snow bursts, were distracting enough to make us stop to appreciate them.

Other plants were into autumn. The Devil's Club stems were as tall as before, but the leaves were yellowing. Some were eaten through. Some were fallen. The ferns were wilting. Their dried out fronds were weak enough to be pulled down by the weight of the fresh rain. Through gaps in the forest, we could see vine maple turning bright red amidst dark evergreens. Leaves and needles fell into a carpet of faded browns, yellows, and greens. Some of that red might also be huckleberry and blueberry leaves turning, but the berry bushes along the trail were green. We didn't get to harvest any because they were all stripped of berries. Whether that was because of a small crop or a thorough hiker's harvest, we didn't know.

Unfortunately, parties had happened. Inside the hollow stumps of trees, and sometimes poorly concealed by bushes, were empty beer cans and wads of toilet paper. Even in protected wilderness or a national park there can be trash, but Barclay is so accessible that the trash is more likely. If you practice overlooking it the trail looks better, but at what point is that deceiving yourself?

A light rain came down before we got to the footbridge and the stream. Our hats kept us dry enough. It would take a monsoon, or weeks of northwest storms, to bring the creek back to life. The trail was quiet because the creek was dry. The few perennially wet pockets along the side and some of the cross streams coming down the hill had running water, but even that was less than last month. The first rains after the dry spell didn't make it to the stream. They had to refill the sponge of the soil. The land was dry and wasn't going to give up rainwater until it had its fill. I wondered how much of that went straight into roots and up into branches.

Some changes were more subtle. The bright orange fungus from last month lasted longer than I expected. It was there, but the color had faded into a brown that blended with the old bark and fallen leaves. I didn't realize mushrooms could last that long.

The bird life was probably different, but sad to say, after twelve months I couldn't identify the different species. Some species must depart the area, but realizing what isn't there is harder than enjoying what is. So few of the birds showed themselves that all I frequently heard was a blended bird song from a chorus of different birds. I liked it, but I couldn't use it to identify anything.

Eventually we met dayhikers leaving. They were the types who get up early and efficiently complete their hike, so they can go home and efficiently complete another noble task. They equipped themselves from the same high end catalog. They were wearing high-tech fabrics and had very new gear. That was good and conservative and safety conscious of them. They were ready for anything. I was wearing a cotton shirt I bought for $13 at a discount store. I save the fancy stuff for overnights and winter hikes. Hiking to a place as close, easy and busy as Barclay simplifies things. There was very little need for extreme gear. I don't advocate stupidity, but I don't ignore advantages either. I could dress simply, so I did. In retrospect, I shouldn't be glib about their attire. I've probably looked like a member of those parties many times. When you don't know what a place is like, dress for safety. I didn't have my same easy attitude the first time I hiked to Barclay, but after a year of visits, I knew when I could relax and when I had to suit up.

The local chipmunks continued their feast of fresh pinecones, or fir cones or whatever they found. Little piles of shredded cones lay in the trail. The cones were pulled apart, so instead of seeing their dark blue green exterior we saw their pink and orange interior. Fall colors show up in the oddest places.

We got to the lake and were surprised to find three tents in place. With the clouds coming in I know that I would have packed and been ready to leave. I also know that I overreact to weather. One party looked relaxed and realistic about the situation. While we sat on a log eating lunch, they sat on the beach playing a card game. Their kids, who might have been ten or twelve, were running around the beach, cruising up the trail, throwing rocks in the water, wearing sticks as swords, and generally acting as kids. Little voices echoed really well from the walls of Baring. They were fun to watch. They weren't malicious, just exuberant.

The lake level was lower and, like I noticed earlier, a small rain wasn't going to suddenly raise it. There was a marsh that had to turn from cracked earth back to mud and then back to marsh. I couldn't even hear the waterfall that helped feed the lake. The drop from last month was probably no more than another foot. The beach grew more than that though because the lake bottom flattens out as it gets shallower. At some point, that must get to be a problem. Neither of us noticed any fish signs. Nothing jumped, but then maybe they were all lying low until the kids went home.

We walked along the beach partly for the fun of it, but also to pick up some trash. A gallon milk jug was adrift on the lake like a tiny runaway iceberg. Kaye retrieved it when the wind blew it to shore. Luckily, there was a chain of driftwood leading across the mud to it; otherwise, she would have had mud up to her knee. When she tried to use her ski pole for support, the pole sunk in without hesitation. The water level was down, but that didn't mean the mud had solidified. The shoreline was pocked with footprints. Some folks enjoyed mucking their way along the shore. She kept her balance, stayed out of the mud and snagged the jug.

At the outlet, we looked at the rings around the lake. The rings marked the various lake levels as it drained. I suspect they each represented one day's loss.

Earlier in the year, the rings along the beach were little six inch terraces. There were about twenty of them and they showed up between two of my visits. The terraces were softened and reduced to a bit of color in the sand that continued across the rocks as parallel lines. Water continued to flow out of the lake, but it wasn't enough to drain it six inches a day anymore. The visible flow at the outlet was far less than what a garden hose can carry.

The summit of Baring was clouded, which was a disappointment. I wanted Kaye to see the peak. The view below it was good enough though. The exposed berry bushes and vine maples showed their autumn oranges and reds bracketed by the grey rocks and green trees. I like the way meadows are framed by trees and rocks in the Cascades. They were framed portraits of autumn.

It was time to get home. Disagreeable tasks like inventorying everything that was stolen, estimating its replacement cost, and unearthing receipts were tasks I wanted to get done before the agents called Monday morning. There were car repairs to get estimated, scheduled and completed. It wasn't the replacement cost that got to me. The insurance would handle that. The time wasted was much more valuable than the stuff stolen and the best insurance policy can't recover time.

I feel much more sympathy for people who lose all their belongings to thieves, natural disasters and accidents. Too much theft is going on and there aren't enough officers to investigate every case. It took too much time to send out an officer to gather fingerprints on my car. The crooks end up with a workable business model because the police have to live within their budgeted sliver of our taxes. The futility of it kicked me into a sour mood. I'd seen it happen at the lake too. There was no way anyone could afford to chase down people who trashed and vandalized the lake and trail. They get away with it and I don't have an easy answer.

That rant sprang to mind as we walked out and it made me realize how my mind works. On the way in, I watched the trail, the flowers, and noticed the birds and the dry streambed. As soon as I thought about heading back to the car, my mind jumped ahead to my to-do list and all those anxieties sprung back full. Heading into nature is far more pleasant for me than heading back into society. Why are the comforts of home not as comforting as the self-inflicted depravations of hiking? Shouldn't all of our laws and technological improvements make life in town more appealing than life without them? Spending hundreds of thousands of dollars on a house and paying taxes for a government should buy a lot more peace of mind. Emotionally it was frustrating, but logically I know that the pleasure I experience in the wild is partly because I don't have to live there long enough for the novelty to wear off. In the long term, the suburban lifestyle wins out, but I grimaced at driving back into it. Nature is a refuge, but realistically it is best taken as a visitor, not a resident.

Having my wife along helped to lessen that dive into a foul mood. She is the real artist at our house and interesting stumps, birdcalls, patches of moss, or lingering berries distracted her, which distracted me. They were all potential inspirations for her sculptures. She pointed out things I overlooked. There were interesting textures and far more subtlety to the colors than what I noticed on my own. Hiking solo has its advantages, but so does hiking with people. By stopping to look at some odd interesting bit, she pulled me out of my downward spiral.

I thought about how different the trail and the forest looked at the end of twelve months. Instead of a line of dirt through a forest, I saw a path built by hard work that wound through, past, and over a string of landmarks and memories. I appreciated the easy walk and missed the river otter. I wondered about the birds and what birders would do to identify those tiny creatures that were hidden in the branches. The trail was a bit too familiar too. I had to stop myself from playing non-stop tour guide to Kaye. She didn't need to hear about what happened at every step of the trail twelve times over.

We got back to the car with no problem and no rain. As we got there, the clouds won the struggle with the sun. The blue sky was gone. The forecast was for five days of rain and a fifteen to twenty degree drop in temperature. Autumn was back a bit ahead of the official schedule and the cycle of the seasons was continuing.

What I Know Now

I now know that Barclay Lake surprised me and that there is a lot more for me to learn there. It was much nicer than I expected from such a near, low, short, flat hike. How many other equally nice places have I overlooked because they seemed too easy? When did easy versus hard become a gauge of pretty versus bland? They really have nothing to do with each other. Barclay Lake was also the first place where I became very aware of how little I know the names and traits of the forest's plants and animals.

The conflicting stories I heard years earlier were all correct, but came from different points of view. It mattered whether someone's single visit was on a day with rain, crowds, or sun, and whether they were there for Barclay Lake, Eagle

Lake, or Baring Mountain. The stories all sounded so different because visiting a place once isn't enough to see and do everything. A year of visits didn't cover all the faces of the place. I never saw the spring flood washing trees downstream. I never saw any of the large local residents like cougar or bear. They probably saw me though. I hadn't even managed a swim in the lake.

I am also glad I did some of my own exploring. Tracking down other folks' old stories would be interesting, but finding stuff on my own like Townsend Mountain made it much more memorable. It made me wonder what else is in that area that could still be explored. I never got to Grotto Lake or Klinger Lake and I haven't checked for routes up Merchant Peak. What was on the other side of Stone Lake, where I heard those voices last fall?

Going to the same place each month had benefits that I appreciated. One hike a month I didn't have to wonder about where to hike. I already had a destination, so there was one less hurdle to cross before I got out the door. After the first trip I rarely needed to worry about driving directions and knew where to stop for breakfast on the way up and lunch on the way back. I could pick a favorite camp-site and have a string of good alternates instead of collapsing onto the first patch of flat open ground. After a few months, I got to play local expert and help other people enjoy the area without having to take classes or get some official certification.

That is probably when I began to feel a bit of ownership for the place. Being able to act as an on-site guide after a few visits helped, but the biggest difference came from helping with the trail maintenance. After that, I had a much greater appreciation for the work involved in letting me hike somewhere. The biggest change wasn't that my ego got stroked but that I looked at my surroundings much more intently instead of breezing on through on the way to checking off another accomplishment

Even the road closure was a worthwhile experience. It proved to me again that the forests the roads cut through are where some of the true wilderness is. I never would have spent time there without the stream undercutting the road. Seeing how our tax dollars get used and how some of us undermine those efforts was a completely different lesson. How can we get ahead when an underfunded Forest Service has to battle nature and irresponsible people? One battle at a time is tough enough.

Barclay Lake was a good place to make me think and wonder about what we should be allowed to do in the forests. Protecting everything can be too limiting. That obliterates freedom and freedom is important in America. Turn that phrase around though and you see the other problem. Total freedom obliterates everything. Total obliteration did not happen, but a forest fire in that area could accomplish that. It was scary seeing evidence of people trying to burn the place down. They had no concept of how catastrophic that would be. We need places that are preserved and places where we can exercise freedom. Barclay Lake sits outside of wilderness protections and isn't in a park, so I suspect it sees more evidence of freedom than lots of places. That level of freedom though is outside my sensibilities. People using the trail for a toilet or trying to start forest fires are carrying that too far. It can happen anywhere, but I am sure it happens there more than in most places. I don't want to see it, but I don't know where the budget would come from that would police the trails. We don't even have enough for the police in town. Nature is largely unprotected from vandals no matter what label we slap on the land.

Despite all those human influences, nature prevails. Left to its own, the forest, the mountains, and the animals would reclaim the area faster than any human restoration job. I expected to see the birds acting more naturally during the middle of the week and they did. The chipmunks acted less naturally during the weekends. Chipmunks showing up for handouts wasn't surprising until I realized that they only did that on the weekends.

No one told me about how dynamic Barclay Lake is. Everyone I talked to had only been there once so they never saw a change in the water level. It was hard for me to miss. Shallows became grasslands. The lake lost half its length. Flood lifted logs got left stacked and dried at the outlet like some monstrous jungle gym. Seeing those stumps of an earlier lake level was also a revelation. The tops of those stumps are at least six to eight feet under water at the end of the rainy season. When did nature build the dam that raised the water and allowed them to drown?

Walking the dried streambed was rare and unforgettable. To see water's convoluted course as it flows around and moves the rocks and the logs is impossible or at least stupidly dangerous at any other time. I've never had such an awesome and rare opportunity to see that bit of nature exposed.

The nearness to Puget Sound-opolis and the presence of the cabin at Eagle Lake makes me wonder when a western slope Cascade resort will be built. It probably won't happen there and the fight at any site will be legendary, but the forces of growth and expansion in the region are immense and can assault from many fronts. Somewhere it will happen. It will be lamented and booked solid. Maybe all of the wild lakes would benefit from one lake acting as a magnet for crowds.

I wanted to see the seasons go by and I succeeded at that, though the road closure tempered that experience. I missed my winter camp.

Barclay Lake is an appealing place. I will be back to revisit it, the nearby lakes and maybe see the stream in flood. I've already tried climbing Baring again, but the weather did not cooperate. Climbing a 6,000 foot peak to look at the inside of a cloud is not the best way to spend a day.

I hope you know and understand Barclay Lake and the area better after having read this book. Some naturalist could do a fine job of cataloging the plants and animals. Hearing from a geologist about the creation of the lake, the cracks in Baring, and the relationship between the various peaks would be a good story. A historian out there probably already knows the story of how people found it and what we've done there over the years. The cabin is worth a book of its own. What you've had though is a simple hiker's view of what is there and I hope I've given you some feeling for what the place is like.

I've described one place for one year. Every year and every place generates a different story. What I experienced only suggests what other stories are out there.

I will continue to visit places for twelve months in a row. Watching the story go by is much more gratifying than the snapshot of a place I get if I only visit it once. I'll still do that too. I like exploring those remote places that are accessible for only a few weeks in the summer. Their views and wildness can be amazing. I hope you find Barclay or your own version. See it now, while you can, and enjoy.

Epilogue

What strange turns the world takes. I wrote this book because I thought people might like reading about a piece of nature in more detail than a guidebook can provide without getting wrapped up in the Latin names of plants or the odd names given to different rocks. So many people can only know a place from their one visit. Some only can read the short description they read in the guidebooks or some scholarly academic text. I had the opportunity to get out there twelve months in a row and write about it, so I did. I had no other agenda than that.

I have opinions though and you've probably noticed a few of them. One of them was about wilderness protections and development. After the book was mostly finished, I learned of "The Wild Sky Wilderness". There was legislation in the US Congress to designate a nice portion of the Cascades as official wilderness. That designation would bring protections and regulations into an area that lacked them. Without intending to, I wrote a book that described a portion of that area. That legislation would change the area I explored.

I am not very political, so I don't know if the legislation passed. If so, then many of the possibilities for protections and developments have been decided. Ironically, I thought that Eagle Lake could get a resort because it already has a cabin there and because a road could be built to the lake. The proposed wilderness boundaries have a squiggle in them that encloses Eagle Lake, then cuts out Barclay Lake, but then turns sharply again to include Baring Mountain. Maybe it won't be that way in the final definition, but there was definite thought put into that map and such contortions don't happen without effort.

Please forgive any aspects that appear dated as a result. I decided to faithfully represent my feelings as they happened rather than rewrite them to fit a cause or to join some winning side. I rarely pick the popular favorite. What you got was me and not the stereotypically tree hugger or resort builder. I don't sit at either of those extremes, and feel that the best answer is somewhere in the middle. I am also not repeating the visits simply to rewrite the book based on the outcome of the legislation. That would be a lot of work, and I sincerely like exploring other places. Besides, the sense of discovery would be lost. I have moved on.

I will be glad to see the area get some protection. It is a very wild area in many ways. To me it is even more precious because it is close to Seattle. Many wilderness areas are safe because they are remote. They are so hard to get to that they almost do not need protection. Nature provides that with tough terrain and conditions. I rarely see litter or vandalism above 6,000 feet. The Wild Sky Wilderness will nicely complement the Alpine Lakes Wilderness that exists on the south side of the highway. They are unique areas and finding their very wet and rugged equivalent outside the Pacific Northwest is difficult.

Maybe a wilderness designation would make it easier for me to learn more about the area. It would be great if the Forest Service published a book that pulled together the naturalist, the geologist and the historian to tell the factual story of not just Barclay, but of the entire Wild Sky Wilderness. I'll look forward to that.

My enthusiasm for the Wilderness continues to be matched by my enthusiasm for an authentic mountain lake lodge on the west side of the Cascades. The resort at Lake Louise in Canada is a very impressive example of one way to do that right. It is a bit highbrow for me, but some folks like that. Getting that built would be tougher than getting legislation passed.

This book is about the changes in nature that are natural and also about those that we inflict upon it. Arguments over legislation won't be the last change the place sees. Seattle grows. Rocks fall. Climates change. The world always changes and any book about it becomes dated as soon as the book is printed. Keep your eyes open because those changes are entertaining and worth watching.

Get out there to enjoy, learn about and respect what is around us.

See you on the trail.

0-595-33114-9

Printed in the United States
22332LVS00005B/251

9 780595 331147